The Trump Challenge
to Black America

The Trump Challenge to Black America

by

Earl Ofari Hutchinson

MID｜DLE PASS｜AGE PRESS

Printed in the United States

Published by
Middle Passage Press
5517 Secrest Drive
Los Angeles, California 90043

Designed by Alan Bell

Publisher's Cataloging-in-Publication data

Names: Hutchinson, Earl Ofari, author.
Title: The Trump challenge to Black America / by Earl Ofari Hutchinson.
Description: Includes bibliographical references and index. | Los Angeles, CA: Middle Passage Press, 2017.
Identifiers: ISBN 978-1881032007
Subjects: LCSH Trump, Donald, 1946- | Presidents—United States—Election—2016. | African Americans—Politics and government—21st century. | Obama, Barack—Influence. | Race—Political aspects—United States. | Racism—Political aspects—United States. | United States—Race relations—Political aspects. | Political participation—United States. | United States—Politics and government—21st century. | United States—Politics and government—2009- | BISAC POLITICAL SCIENCE / American Government / Executive Branch | SOCIAL SCIENCE / Discrimination & Race Relations | POLITICAL SCIENCE / Civil Rights
Classification: LCC E185.615 .H88 2017 | DDC 305.896/073—dc23

Table of Contents

The Trump Challenge
to Black America

Introduction

It was a surreal moment and an even more surreal statement when President-elect Donald Trump met with two legendary African-American football players, Jim Brown and Ray Lewis at Trump Tower on December 16, 2016. This was five weeks after his election. The surreal moment was the meeting itself. Lewis and Brown were lambasted, vilified, and harangued by many blacks as sell-outs, traitors, Uncle Toms and much worse. They drew intense heat because they dared to meet with the man who black voters universally loathed.

The surreal statement came from Brown who rashly told a *CNN* interviewer immediately after the meeting that he "loved" and admired Trump. This was regarded as worse than heresy. To many critics, it was tantamount to aiding and abetting a sworn enemy. Brown later walked back his "love" Trump statement by chalking it up to a typo. He was clearly reacting to the backlash he got from daring to meet with Trump.

Brown and Lewis were hardly the only prominent blacks to meet with Trump before, during and after the presidential campaign and his election. The parade of black preachers, businesspersons, professionals, athletes and entertainers that either trooped to Trump Tower, or met with him in highly staged and orchestrated venues, was nothing short of breath taking. It was breath taking because he ran the most vicious, unabashed, race baiting, Muslim, and immigrant baiting campaign since state's rights presidential candidate Alabama governor George Wallace in 1964.

Brown and the parade of blacks who met with Trump soft pedaled their meeting with him. Their standard retort was that he is the president and that it is foolhardy to bury their heads in the sand and deny that reality, unpleasant as it might be. They noted that there were millions of dollars in contracts, business and professional opportunities, administration appointments, vital federal job, education, health and civil rights protection programs at stake with the Trump administration. There was simply no way to ignore that.

They had an unarguable point. As loathsome as Trump was to most blacks, he would be at the federal helm for at least four years. This was a lot of time to wreak irreparable program and institutional damage to those programs.

* * * * *

The meeting with Trump, though, didn't address two gaping problems that told much about the rocky road that blacks would tread with Trump. Brown typified the first problem. After marching out of Trump Tower, he made absolutely no mention of anything that Trump specifically said or did to assure that he'd commit to any specific program or initiative, or provide added resources that would boost Brown's at-risk youth program, amer-I-Can.

That also applied to dozens of other programs in poor, inner city neighborhoods that mentor, tutor, and provide family support services to at-risk youth. The bulk of these programs are run on a shoe string budget and are one step away from closing their doors. Other than Brown gushing over Trump, there was stone silence from

Trump about what, if anything, he had to offer in return for the love fest Brown, Lewis and other blacks who met with him showed him.

This was even stranger since Trump never tired of boasting during the campaign that he was a negotiator. So, if Brown, and the other blacks who flocked to him had done some hard bargaining with him to get his administration to commit to specific programs to aid the black poor and black businesses, then the meeting with him would have made some sense. That would have put Trump on record and on the spot to deliver on the commitment. If he reneged he would be shown up for the congenital liar that many considered him to be. Brown got a few seconds of face time on the news, and Trump got a chance to boast again that there were a lot of blacks who liked him. Yet, the record showed in the months after the meeting, Trump did not deliver on a single item that would have benefited Brown and others that ran programs in their communities.

The other problem with the photo-op meetings blacks had with Trump was that they met with him at almost the very moment when he was stuffing his administration with the greatest array of generals, military men, and billionaires of any administration in American history. His picks to head the Education Department, Labor Department, Housing and Urban Development, Health, Education and Welfare, the Small Business Administration, and especially the Justice Department, had a long history of warfare against the very programs that these departments administer. Those programs provide the vast array of resources, support, and protections for poor, working class blacks.

In fact, Trump's initial cabinet, stocked with mostly white males, and only one token Hispanic and black, Ben Carson, HUD Secretary, was the whitest presidential cabinet since Ronald Reagan's cabinets in the 1980s. His big four, and most prestigious and policy influential cabinet posts, the attorney general, and the secretaries of state, treasury and defense, were conservative, corporate grounded, white males.

A textbook example of that was that the day after Brown met with Trump, it was revealed that Commerce Department secretary-designate billionaire Wilbur Ross cheer led 2012 GOP presidential contender Mitt Romney's ill-informed and racial pandering quip in 2012 that 47 percent of Americans are free loaders on the government. Their alleged sponging on the government came presumably at the expense of the tax paying middle and upper class.

The Commerce Department is charged with overseeing the Minority Business Development Agency which is tasked with providing resources and support for minority businesses. These are the businesses that Brown and other blacks endlessly implore presidents to boost spending on. If you had a Commerce head that thought most non-whites sole role in life is to have their hand out at the government trough, then it didn't take much imagination to see what minority entrepreneurs might expect from his department.

During the campaign, Trump tailored the few pitches he made to blacks for their votes to reflect the stock GOP pro-business, free enterprise and the healthy economy line as something that blacks also could and should embrace. Brown and the other black Trump admirers took that message to heart. The question is, did Trump? Neither Brown or the other blacks who met with him had an answer to that question. African-Americans would have four years to find out. This was the great challenge of Trump's presidency to Black America.

In the three-year period from 2015 to 2017, I covered and analyzed every aspect of the speeches, utterances, and positions Trump posited during his presidential campaign on health care, civil rights, voting rights, criminal justice and police abuse, education, and President Obama in my featured columns in the *Huffington Post*. My special emphasis was on the issues that most affected African-Americans that a Trump candidacy and presidency would impact. Those issues are health, education jobs, the criminal justice system, and race relations as. *The Trump Challenge to Black America* is based on those columns. I have expanded those columns with added material, fresh assessments, and a detailed look at the direction Trump has taken the country in since his election. The conclusion is the same as in my columns. Trump poses the greatest challenge and peril of any president in modern times to black Americans. I work through for the reader not only his positions on the issues and how they imperil African-Americans but, equally important, what can be done to combat the peril.

CHAPTER 1

Racial Pandering to and in The White House

In November 2016, GOP presidential candidate Trump was in full, aggressive, take-no-prisoners campaign mode as he heart-edly cheered on a crowd at a campaign rally in Birmingham, Alabama. His cheerleading was not in response to the almost exclusively white, raucous crowd showing their wild enthusiasm for him. It was in reaction to the assault by some in the crowd on a black protester. Later in the day in an interview on *Fox News*, Trump was unapologetic. He called the protester's action disgusting, and said, "Maybe he should have been roughed up."

He promptly followed that up with a tweet that blatantly doctored up black crime figures which were so racist that even some staunch conservatives cringed at the ploy. They didn't buy his lame, partial, walk back excuse that he later gave when confronted with the true figures on crime. He said that he was simply retweeting what a supporter sent him.

Trump was oblivious to the criticism for a good reason. His naked racial pandering and baiting was a big part of what rocket launched him to the front of the GOP presidential pack almost from the moment he officially announced his candidacy in June 2015 with his stock campaign slogan, "We are going to make America great again." His emphasis on making the country great again was an open signal to many fearful whites that the country was on a hell bent downward spiral and the blame for that lay squarely on pushy blacks, minorities, immigrants and gays.

Trump's race-baiting was hardly new. The instant a multi-million-dollar settlement was announced in 2014 with the five young African-American and Latino youths falsely convicted and imprisoned for assault and rape of a jogger in New York's Central Park in 1989, Trump loudly ranted against the settlement. He did everything possible to whip up another round of racial hysteria over the case. And why not? When the case broke in 1989, he had shelled out $85,000 to four newspapers to splash an ad demanding the death penalty for the five. The legal exoneration of the men and the overwhelming evidence that they were innocent meant nothing to Trump.

The case more than any other single occurrence moved Trump from being just another plodding, conniving, business magnate to a coming figure on the political scene. Race baiting the Central Park Five made Trump a political player. It also taught him a lesson that racial demagogues have known for ages. The lesson from this was how a demagogue could take a racially volatile issue loaded with hysteria and emotion and twist, bend, and fracture it into an ego, name and attention getting device to move up the political food chain. Trump hit political pay dirt in race baiting with the Central Park Five case, and he never looked back.

* * * * *

By that time, Trump's line of naked bigotry in the case had taken on a life of its own. In October 1973, he was ripped by the Justice Department for blatant racial discrimination in his apartment rentals. When cornered on his racist exclusion, he blithely said that if he didn't his other tenants (meaning white tenants) would flee from his units and the city.

This was only a warm-up for the racial antic that turned him from a wheeler dealer real estate investor, blustery casino owner, and reality TV producer, into a political household name. This was the thinly disguised racist savaging of President Obama when he floated the notion of a presidential campaign in 2012. He did that by stoking hard the phony, fraudulent and bigoted Birther movement. This held that Obama was not an American citizen and therefore was ineligible to be President. Then he doubled down on that by demanding that Obama produce his supposed doctored college transcripts.

Trump knew that while the issue had been thoroughly discredited and disavowed by every leading GOP presidential candidate in 2012, a significant number, if not a majority of Republicans, actually believed or wanted to believe that Obama's birth was a legitimate issue to dump back on the political table. The resulting avalanche of lawsuits and petitions filed in various state courts that contested Obama's U.S. citizenship showed there was some mileage Trump could gain by continuing to wave the issue around.

The pay-off was that he conned enough newsrooms, talk show hosts and legions of the GOP's inveterate Obama bashers to chat up a Trump presidential candidacy. Trump got what he wanted. That was tons of fresh media attention, a momentary seat at the GOP presidential candidate's chat table, and starry-eyed idolization from legions of ultra-conservatives and untold numbers of unreconstructed bigots.

Ever on the alert for an angle to race bait or to apologize for racism, he piled on the bandwagon in April 2014 to defend former Los

Angeles Clipper owner Donald Sterling. Sterling was caught on tape making racist rants. Trump didn't criticize Sterling for making racist remarks. Instead, he finger-pointed the Clipper's owner's girlfriend for allegedly "setting him up."

There was one major difference in how Trump used open race baiting to get national and political attention and what legions of other GOP presidential candidates and presidents from Nixon to George W. Bush, and GOP state and local candidates and elected officials did. His was blatant and in-your-face baiting. The other GOP president's racial baiting was subtle, sneaky and loaded with emotional hot button code words and phrases that were designed to stoke the racial fires to win and maintain office. These GOP presidents knew that it was not necessary to make overt mention of race to tug at the emotional strings of the GOP's core constituency—white conservative, rural and blue-collar workers. A wink and a nod with code words on welfare cheats, entitlements, tax and spend big government, and immigrants, and the endless wedge issues from gay marriage to abortion was more than enough to boost their poll ratings among their base supporters.

Trump's racial savaging was different. It had a hard, bitter and overtly dangerous edge to it. Worse, it hit at the right time. Polls showed that millions of whites were wracked with worry, concern, were edgy and fearful about the future and the direction of the country. This was layered over with the horrid thought of their losing grip on their numbers and power to blacks, Hispanics, gays, women, and immigrants. The usual standardized code words and phrases that GOP establishment politicians had worked so well in the past could not compete with a good old-fashioned appeal to black crime, Muslim bashing, and a call to send them all packing back across the border. Trump proved that he was the right man to say just that and reap a big reward in the process. This was especially the case on the issue that has always been the surest fire conservative shibboleth and conservative audience pleaser that harked back to Nixon. That was law order and black crime.

* * * * *

Trump's venue, the audience and the timing in September 2016 was perfect to make that pitch. He chose to cast himself firmly as the law and order presidential candidate. The venue was a town hall style campaign rally in suburban Cleveland Heights, Ohio. The audience was, as nearly always the case with Trump's frenzied audiences, virtually lily white. The timing to make his law and order pitch came after several highly publicized, and controversial police shootings of young black men in Tulsa, Oklahoma and Charlotte, North Carolina. An audience member rose to ask him just what he'd do to check crime and violence in black communities. Trump was ready, "One of the things I'd do," he said, "is I would do stop-and-frisk. I think you have to. We did it in New York, it worked incredibly well and you have to be proactive."

The audience as if on cue exploded with thunderous applause. Trump wasn't finished. He then piled on with the litany of stereotypes and distortions about alleged black crime. He cited the murder surge in Chicago, and other big cities. It could be stopped with a big crack down. Stop and frisk was his answer. There were two problems with Trump's hearty embrace of stop and frisk. The first was that the stop and frisk tactic during the years police used it with reckless abandon in New York criminalized virtually a whole generation of young black men. The statistics on it told the blatantly racist tale of stop and frisk.

In the near decade from 2004 to 2012, the NYPD used stop and frisk, more than 80 percent of the stops were of blacks and Hispanics. The majority of the stops did not result in the confiscation of guns, or other weapons. In many cases, the charges, if any were ever filed, were later dropped. Yet, their names were on police files. The tactic was such a naked racial targeting ploy that a federal judge called a halt to it in 2013. He flatly called it what it was, an outrageous infringement on the rights of minorities. As for the claim that it reduced gun crime and violence in New York and other cities, there was no evidence to support that stop and frisk alone had anything to do with the reduction. Gun violence and crime dropped in many cities nationally during that period. Not one of those cities had anything close to the unabashed use of stop and frisk shakedowns of young blacks and Hispanics as in New York.

Yet, a non-perturbed Trump, either ignorant of that fact, or more likely knowing full well that it didn't do much to reduce crime, but had immeasurable political value to rev up his mostly white crowds, was defiant. He later tweeted, "NYC politicians better stop pandering—ending stop & frisk would be a disaster."

* * * * *

Trump's stop and frisk gambit fit in with his larger political strategy. That was to reach back nearly a half century and steal the script that Nixon used in his successful 1968 presidential election bid. Trump now in full Nixon mode christened himself the "law and order candidate." This touched another nerve with Trump leaning white voters. Polls showed in the three states that would likely decide the 2016 presidential election, Ohio, Florida, and Pennsylvania, Trump surged either edge close to Democratic rival Hillary Clinton or drew to a statistical dead heat with her.

In 1968, Nixon was brutal and direct when he said that the "solution to the crime problem is not the quadrupling of funds for any governmental war on poverty but more convictions." There it was. Forget spending money on jobs, education, and social programs to aid the ghetto poor and reduce crime, the real answer was simply more police and prisons, and put a man in the White House who was willing to say and do just that.

It was cold, calculating and cynical, but it worked. Law and order resuscitated the career of Nixon, the man many saw as a hopelessly failed, flawed, has been politician. It turned him into the front-runner for the White House in 1968. He ridiculed the thought that poverty, racial discrimination and social inequities were the root cause of crime, violence and ghetto unrest. Nixon doubled down on this with a thinly disguised Southern Strategy in which he did a hard court of fearful blue-collar whites and, unreconstructed racists in the South. He piled on a healthy dose of racially loaded code words such as "out of control big government," "welfare cheats," "permissiveness," and "crime in the streets." This pitch gave Nixon a comfortable lead in the polls over his Democratic rival Hubert Humphrey for much of the campaign.

Trump almost certainly knew that history. By swiping Nixon's law and order line, he opened yet another attack thread for the campaign. He had plenty to play on that summer. There was the heinous slaying of the five Dallas police officers in July 2016, and the fear and the rage at the killings. The subtle ingredients of racial hysteria were there to try and make the law and order pitch stick. There was an African-American shooter, who allegedly made anti-white utterances, five dead white police officers, and a convenient whipping boy movement, Black Lives Matter. BLM conjured up for many a nihilistic, anti-white, anti-police, lawless group of blacks.

The difference between how Nixon stoked the racist passions in

1968 and what Trump did in 2016 was that it was not the South that Trump aimed to make his law and order sell too. It was nervous, fearful voters in the swing states, and conservative independents. They were the ones Trump banked on to tip the scales in these states in his direction.

*   *   *   *   *

He also had another foil. That was to tar the Democrats as a party, and Clinton as a candidate, that tilted and pandered shamelessly to minorities, particularly blacks, by allegedly fueling anti-police sentiment, with its kid glove approach to Black Lives Matter. Democrats and Clinton allegedly made things even worse by relentlessly pushing for more spending on job, health and education programs. The strong hint was that this was all done at the expense of hard working, law abiding, white middle class and blue-collar workers.

The law and order sounding got even more resonance in this era with the cable TV network's 24-hour news cycle that was filled with continual feeds of street protests against police abuse, complete with taunts, curses and shouts at police officers. The image portrayed was one of a country bursting at the seams, and that was so hopelessly racially polarized that it would take nothing less than a full-blown police crackdown to correct things. It might also require even bigger spending on weaponry and military preparedness by police to deal with the supposed anarchy in the streets.

In 1968, Nixon got his way on all counts by wrapping himself in the mantel of law and order. He edged out Humphrey. He shifted the public's and the federal government's focus to beefing up resources for a wild expansion of police power and a prison building boom. He finger-pointed liberal Democrats for their emphasis on more social programs to deal with the plight of the urban poor. Worst of all, he virtually encoded the blame the victim narrative into the public mind for the very poverty and abuse that gave rise to the urban unrest in the first place. Trump pretty much stuck to the same script. The polls that put him neck and neck with Clinton in the must win states were a stark reminder that presidential history often repeated itself.

When Trump self-proclaimed himself the "law and order candidate", the "stop and frisk" candidate "the stop black crime and murder" candidate he knew it would hit home. They were the ancient and durable racist code words and slogans that arch race baiters have used seemingly forever too tap the raw, racial nerve of millions.

Trump was now in the White House. Eyes would now nervously watch to see how Trump would translate his campaign slogans and pitches for toughness on black crime, unconditional support for the police, a ramp up in more military hardware for the police, and a rejection of the Obama administration's efforts at criminal justice reform and fairness, into White House policy. The future on this score did not bode well for blacks.

* * * * *

Whether it was law and order, or Trump refusing to denounce former Klan Kleagle David Duke's endorsement, nor any other support from the Klan, Trump stood firmly on ground that had been well-trodden by legions of GOP candidates at all levels, and that included GOP presidents and presidential candidates. This was to make racial pandering a powerful political weapon to either win or be competitive in elections.

On a cable talk show appearance in July 2010, Senate Minority Leader Mitch McConnell flatly refused several direct, angled, and nuanced efforts to discuss racism in the Tea Party. McConnell's none too subtle refusal to weigh in on the issue was in direct response to an NAACP resolution at its annual convention that month that demanded that the Tea Party speak out, and speak out loudly against the racists among them.

McConnell was silent on the racism issue for a good reason. Since the 1964 presidential election, the GOP had employed an arsenal of racist code words and slogans to energize the party's traditional conservative, white male loyalists, and increasingly white female supporters. The 2008 presidential election gave ample warning of that. While Obama made a major breakthrough in winning a significant percent of votes from white independents and young white voters, McCain (not Obama) won a slim majority of their vote in the final tally. Overall, Obama garnered slightly more than 40 percent of the white male vote. Among white male voters in the South and heartland, Obama made almost no impact. Overall, McCain garnered nearly 60 percent of the white vote.

The GOP could not have been competitive during the 2008 and 2012 presidential campaigns without the bailout from white male voters. Much has been made since 2012 that these voters were a dwindling percent of the electorate, and that Hispanics, Asian, black, young, and women voters will permanently tip the balance of political power to the Democrats in coming national elections. Blue collar white voters have shrunk from more than half of the nation's voters to less than 40 percent.

GOP leaders have long known that blue collar and a significant percent of college educated, white male voters, who are professionals can be easily aroused to vote and shout loudly on the emotional wedge issues; abortion, family values, anti-gay marriage and tax cuts. They whipped up their hysteria and borderline racism against the Affordable Care Act, and by extension Obama when he as in office.

This was glaringly apparent in the ferocity and bile spouted by the shock troops the GOP leaders in consort with the Tea Party activists brought out to harangue, harass and bully Democrat legislators on the eve of the health care vote in 2010. These were the very voters that GOP presidents and aspiring presidents, Nixon, Reagan, Bush Sr. and George W. Bush, McCain and Romney, and an endless line of GOP governors, senators and congresspersons banked on for victory and to seize and maintain regional and national political dominance.

Trump studied the template well. Along the way, he managed to add a few tweaks to it. There was his swagger and bluster, his tough talk on crime, his non-stop assault on Obama, his thinly disguised appeal to violence against protesters, and his patronizing attitude toward blacks. Trump would never soften his stance during the campaign on these points. And he showed no sign of softening once in the White House. The same could be said of the GOP.

CHAPTER 2

Trump's
Black Outreach

In the span of less than two weeks during the first week of September 2016, GOP presidential candidate Trump did something that few thought possible, let alone desirable. He went to not one, but two black churches in Detroit and in Flint, Michigan. Now at first glance, that seemed to fly in the face of everything that he said and stood for. Up to that point he had spent virtually his entire campaign nakedly and hideously spouting every kind of racist, anti-black, anti-Obama slur, dig, taunt and finger-point. He had a vile history of race baiting—the Central Park Five, defying repeated federal government housing agency demands to rent to blacks, virtually blaming Obama for the Baltimore riots in 2015, and flatly refusing to address any black group.

Now here was Trump at the two churches beaming in their pulpits. He was embraced by a coterie of black ministers, prayer worshippers, and assorted other black curiosity seekers. The idea behind Trump's church tour was simple. It was a campaign stage-managed act to show that he was not a racist. The black church was the key to making the act work. The prime reason Trump chose the church venue was that GOP candidates had used this tact before.

In the 2004 presidential election campaign, GOP strategists discovered that conservative black evangelicals could be a very willing and pliant audience. Though the majority of black churchgoers still voted by a huge majority for Democratic presidential candidate John Kerry in that election, they gave GOP rival George Bush the cushion he needed to bag Ohio and remain in the White House. There were early warning signs that might happen. The same polls showed black's prime concern was with bread and butter issues. Kerry was viewed as the candidate who could deliver on those issues. Yet, they also revealed that a sizeable number of blacks ranked abortion, gay marriage, and school prayer as priority issues. Their concern for these issues didn't come anywhere close to that of white evangelicals. However, it was still higher than that of the general voting public.

In the right place and under the right circumstance, black evangelicals posed a stealth danger to Democrats. As it turned out, the right place for Bush was Ohio, Wisconsin, and Florida. These were must-win swing states, and Bush won them with a considerably higher percent of the black vote than he got in 2000. In Ohio, the gay marriage ban helped bump up the black vote for Bush by seven percentage points, to 16 percent. In Florida and Wisconsin, Republicans aggressively courted and wooed key black religious leaders. They dumped big bucks from Bush's Faith-Based Initiative program into church-run education and youth programs. Black church leaders not only endorsed Bush, but in some cases, they actively worked for his re-election, and encouraged members of their congregations to do the same.

* * * * *

The lesson of the 2004 campaign wasn't lost on Trump. He quickly grabbed a few hand-picked prominent black evangelicals for a much-touted meeting, and photo-op at Trump Tower in December 2015. Some of the preachers there endorsed Trump, some said they just wanted to hear more from him. Others quickly distanced themselves from him. That was less important than the fact that Trump could show the world that not all blacks hated his guts and would do anything to make sure the closest he ever got to the White House was on a guest tour pass.

The black ministers who showed up at the gathering more than fit the image massage he wanted. In the weeks afterwards, a few more black ministers said they'd back Trump. A few went further and turned up on the network talk shows singing his praises.

This was all a prelude to the big camp meetings in Detroit, and now Flint. In both places, a heckle or two notwithstanding, Trump got exactly what he wanted, a mostly attentive, respectful, audience that took his empty platitudes about civil rights in stride.

* * * * *

At that stage of the presidential campaign in the summer of 2016, it was more important than ever for Trump to make some effort to soften his well-earned and deserved image as the most racist candidate to mount a presidential campaign since George Wallace in 1964. There was great laughter and knowing nods when some polls showed that Trump would get 0 percent of the black vote. This seemed about right. Trump earned and deserved the goose egg with his horrendous race baiting record. However, a funny thing happened between the near gag line 0 percent Trump supposedly would get if the election were held in July 2016, and the actual election. That 0 percent of the black vote magically transformed into some real numbers that actually had some significance for the election, and maybe beyond when the polls closed and Trump was the President-Elect. The transformation went from the earlier 0 percent showing to 8 percent of the black vote. Numbers wise that factored out to roughly a half million votes. That topped the total that GOP presidential contenders Romney in 2012 and McCain in 2008 got. Another 4 percent of black voters did not support Clinton. Together, that was over 1 million black votes lost to Clinton. That raised eyebrows.

The drop off in the black vote for Clinton from what Obama got was easy to explain. One, she was not Obama. He was black and his campaign became a virtual holy crusade by blacks to make history and put one of their own in the White House. No white Democrat could hope to match that spine-tingling exuberance. A lot more blacks repeatedly ripped and nagged at Clinton for Bill Clinton's alleged racial sins as president. Those alleged sins were his shove through of the draconian omnibus crime bill that soared the numbers of blacks in federal and, by extension, state prisons; and a welfare reform bill that seemed more punitive than helpful. Hillary's own one-time offensive branding of black lawbreakers as "super predators" also hurt her.

However, the harsh reality was that thousands of blacks did vote for Trump. Their reasons were just as easy to explain. Trump touched a tiny nerve with his shout that poor, underserved black neighborhoods are supposedly a mess with lousy public schools, high crime and violence, and chronic joblessness and poverty. He dumped the blame for that squarely on the Democrats who run and have run most of these cities for decades. This was just enough to take the hard and sharp edge for some blacks off the almost-set-in-stone image of Trump as a guy with a white sheet under his suit.

In 2008 and 2012, black GOP advocacy groups ran ads hammering the Democrats again for their alleged indifference to and outright aid and abet of black suffering in the inner cities. They touted the GOP's emphasis on small business, school choice, and family values as the best path to black advancement. This pitch has always had some appeal to many blacks. Though it would never trigger any kind of stampede to the GOP by even most of these conservative-leaning blacks, it was enough to take some of the sting out of the GOP's long history of racial abuse.

Trump understood enough of that history. He tailored the few raw appeals he made to blacks for their votes to reflect the standard GOP pro-business, free enterprise, and the healthy economy line as something that blacks also could and should embrace.

The 8 percent of blacks who voted for Trump, combined with the numbers who didn't vote at all, or didn't vote for Clinton, did not help elect Trump. He won with an Obama like crusade among less educated white male and female, blue collar and rural voters. However, enough blacks did buy his claim that a conservative, Republican businessman, with a horrific tainted racial history, was a better bet in the Oval Office than a Democrat. This made Trump's victory even more of a troubling political oddity and challenge.

* * * * *

The challenge was plainly evident in November 2016 when former BET founder and financial mogul Bob Johnson trooped to Trump Tower. After the meeting, he urged African-Americans to give President-Elect Trump a "shot" and "the benefit of the doubt." Johnson was hectored with a slew of printable and unprintable epitaphs from many blacks who raged at him for daring to say such a thing. Johnson didn't damp down the anger when he claimed that he turned down a Trump offer of an administration post. The check list of anti-Trump reasons for their rage at Johnson for his "benefit of the doubt" admonition was by then well known.

In the weeks after his election, Trump did absolutely nothing to change the perception that his administration would be a relentless foe of civil rights, public education and expanded health programs. He nominated a sworn enemy of civil and voting rights to the Attorney General post, Jeff Sessions, an avowed foe of public education to the education post, Betsy DeVos, and did not back away from his plan to repeal Obamacare.

So, what then possessed Johnson to say Trump deserved a chance? Johnson is rich, influential and corporate and politically well-connected. He's among the one percent of businesspersons who Trump feels comfortable with, and surrounds himself with. He has the kind of access to Trump that few blacks or anyone else not in the mogul's class could even in their wildest dreams imagine.

The proof was Johnson's face to face with Trump and a purported offer of a job in his administration. It was easy for Johnson to imagine that since Trump was willing to meet and talk with him he might be willing to do the same with other blacks. Johnson didn't make any reference to it after the meeting. Trump, however, did put on the policy table during the campaign what he branded a ten-point plan for blacks, promising greater job creation, safe communities, business investment, and equal justice.

* * * * *

Whether Trump would do any of this during his administration was less important than that he put it on paper. This gave the appearance that he was at least thinking about the problems of the inner cities and posed what he considered solutions to those problems. There was just enough there for Johnson and an undetermined number of other African-Americans, particularly businesspersons, professionals, and ministers, to take a step back and wait and see if Trump would go anywhere with this plan. This was even more plausible considering that Trump made a better showing among black voters than Romney or McCain in their presidential bids. Legions of other blacks either didn't vote for or raged at Clinton for her alleged political sins. The far bigger reason that Johnson wanted blacks to go easy on Trump, at least in the beginning, was hard political reality. He was the President. He would be in the Oval Office for at least four years. This was a classic case of real politick for Johnson; railing against Trump wouldn't make that go away.

That brought it back to Johnson's contention that Trump was the President and he was not going away. Therefore, it was incumbent on African-American leaders and organizations to find possible areas of agreement with him on some issues. The greater goal being, if not to get an increase in job, health and education spending, then at least to prevent Trump from a wholesale hack up or scrap of these programs.

This was not a new conundrum. Civil rights groups faced the same problem and dilemma with Reagan and George W. Bush. Both were conservative Republicans who stacked their administration deck with many ultra-conservatives who had their sights set on gutting programs. They were bent on a conservative overhaul of the federal government and the courts.

Civil rights groups had a dual approach to Reagan and Bush. They waged relentless battle with both administrations on voting rights, Supreme Court appointments; and against draconian slashes in health, education and jobs programs. At the same time, when the opportunity presented itself, they met with both presidents to keep the lines of communication open.

Johnson's point was that if blacks warred with Trump or put

their hands over their eyes and pretended he didn't exist, then that insured he'd do the same with African-Americans. It was a valid point. The problem was that no matter how much of a chance Johnson and African-Americans were prepared to give Trump, there was no guarantee he'd ever return the favor. And much reason to believe that he wouldn't.

CHAPTER 3

Trump's Injustice Department

F ew Attorney Generals to be ever, gave a more chilling preview of how the federal government would pick and choose what federal laws to enforce or ignore once he assumed the reins as the nation's top law enforcement officer than Alabama Senator Jeff Sessions. He did just that in his long and very public stances on civil rights, criminal justice and voting rights issues over the years.

The preview of what could be expected from him once he assumed the post of Attorney General came in 2008 when the Alabama Policy Institute published a position paper on what it considered a dangerous trend by the courts and attorneys general. The trend was the court's approval of consent decrees. For decades, consent decrees have been major weapons wielded by the Justice Department to go after cities, states, and corporations that engage in blatant abusive practices on everything from consumer fraud to police abuse.

The Institute compiled a lengthy position paper that railed against the use of consent decrees to right wrongs. It demanded that attorneys general and state legislatures act to limit, if not outright do away with, the use of consent decrees. The Institute asked the one attorney general whom it was certain would back its conclusions to the hilt to write the introduction. U.S. Senator Jeff Sessions got right to the point in the very first two sentences, "One of the most dangerous, and rarely discussed exercises of raw power is the issuance of expansive court decrees. They have a profound effect on our legal system as they constitute an end around the democratic process." He boasted that as Alabama Attorney General he rushed to the courts to scrap a consent decree approved by his predecessor. He bragged that he succeeded. Sessions heartily cheered the Institute for leading the charge to curtail the use of consent decrees.

GOP senators, conservative bloggers, and legal shills during Session's Senate confirmation hearings for the Attorney General post launched a charm campaign to paint him as a guy who had been misunderstood. His racially demeaning quotes supposedly were taken out of context and, as Alabama Attorney General and later, U.S. Attorney, he had urged vigorous prosecution of a Klan murderer, backed school desegregation efforts, filed lawsuits against voting rights discrimination, and backed the extension of the Voting Rights Act in 2006.

* * * * *

That was simply PR puffery and window dressing to mask the extreme peril Sessions posed once he was in the saddle at the U.S. Justice Department. There were glaring signs that he would not play by the legal and public interest book as Attorney General. During the 2016 presidential campaign, he claimed that he didn't see any criminal act in Trump's boast that he grabbed women in their private parts. This struck to the heart of whether Sessions' Justice Department would deal impartially with vital Department gender enforcement issues such as support for marriage equality, pay equity for women, and domestic violence, and sexual assault.

He also didn't object when Trump said he'd prosecute Hillary Clinton and investigate Black Lives Matter. Then there was the question of just what types of crimes Sessions would prosecute. There are an estimated 4000 federal criminal statutes on the books that could be subject to prosecution. It's up to the Attorney General to decide which crimes to make a priority for prosecution. Holder and Lynch put the department spotlight on protecting immigration rights, voting rights, police abuse, drug and criminal justice system reform, and doing away with the use of private prisons for profit. Sessions chomped to get rid of voting rights enforcement, calling the Voting Rights Act "intrusive."

As for private prisons, under former Attorney General Eric Holder, the Bureau of Prisons issued a memo that it would phase out the use of private, for-profit prisons, citing grave problems in safety, security, and oversight. During the campaign, Trump disagreed, calling for even more privatizations and private prisons. Geo Group is one of the largest private prison corporations. Four months after Trump advocated private prisons, in October 2016, the GEO Group saw the pro privatization handwriting on the wall and hired two former Sessions aides to lobby in favor of outsourcing federal corrections to private contractors.

* * * * *

There was yet another sign of the shape of things to come at the Justice Department under Sessions. In 1997, when he was Alabama's Attorney General, a state judge went after him, calling him and his office an example of perpetrating the "worst case" of prosecutorial misconduct he had seen. The case that got the judge up in arms against Sessions was a prosecution of a trucking company for allegedly submitting fraudulent billings and taking kickbacks. Specifically, the charge was that his office failed to turn over evidence, gave false testimony, and abused the defendant's rights. Subsequent rulings and an ethics commission investigation found no wrong doing on Sessions' part. However, there was a taint with the public charge that Sessions, as the judge noted, was willing to "disregard the lawful duties of the Attorney General."

There were certainly precedents where prior Attorney Generals went against the prevailing philosophy and wishes of the man who appointed him or her, namely the President. However, Sessions had been in public life for decades. There was absolutely no hint, based on his Senate voting record, public statements and actions, and ties to hard right-wing groups, that once in the Justice Department saddle, that he would suddenly be a fair and impartial enforcer of civil rights laws, voting rights, and a supporter of criminal justice reforms.

Trump and GOP leaders knew exactly what they were getting with Sessions. They quickly made it clear that they would do everything politically possible to get him in the post.

* * * * *

So, it was no accident that GOP Senate Judiciary Committee Chairman Chuck Grassley speed dialed the confirmation hearings of Sessions before Trump officially took office in January 2017. It was no accident that he has ignored all entreaties from skeptical Democratic Senators to delay the hearings. It was also no accident that the GOP made no issue of Session's nominee questionnaire that cabinet picks were required to submit before confirmation hearings. His questionnaire had more gaping holes than Swiss cheese.

Sessions was the GOP's long-awaited point man to fulfill the GOP's longest and fondest dream. That is its total domination of the national electorate. With that, the GOP would have a virtual lock on the federal government for years to come. To make that happen, the GOP would have to continue to discourage and damp down the number of minority and poor voters who can register to vote and who overwhelmingly vote Democratic. This entailed ramming through a rash of naked voter suppression laws, initiatives, and stumbling blocks. The first wave of these laws came after the presidential election in 2000 and the disputed ballot count between Bush and Gore in Florida. The trend to restrict voting accelerated between the mid-term elections in 2010 and 2014. GOP dominated state legislatures enacted laws requiring rigid voter IDs, a big scale back in voting hours, limiting, if not ending, weekend voting, drastically restricting the number of polling places and registrars in minority neighborhoods, and banning felon voting.

* * * * *

The second step was to saber rattle the landmark 1965 Voting Rights Act. The GOP floated several trial balloons in Congress. The first one was in 1981 when the Act came up for renewal. The deal in the initial passage of the Act was that it be renewed every 25 years. A few hardline ultraconservatives in the administration of then President Reagan administration made some loud threats to push Reagan to oppose its renewal. Reagan signed the renewal legislation. When the Act came up for renewal again in 2006, a pack of House Republicans stalled the legislation for more than a week and demanded that hearings be held. Bush eventually signed the renewal order.

This opened the gate for the next step; take it to the Supreme

Court. Three days after President Obama's reelection in 2012, GOP conservatives demanded that the Court scrap the centerpiece of the Act, Section 5. That was the provision that mandated that states get "preclearance" from the Justice Department before making any changes in voting procedures. The court did.

This wasn't enough. The Voting Rights Act is still on the federal books. As long as it is, it must be enforced. This puts it squarely in the lap of the Justice Department and the Attorney General. When the Justice Department was in the hands of Obama's Attorney General Holder, there was no cause for concern. In countless speeches and interviews, Holder made it clear that he would do everything within his department's power to enforce the law to protect and, where possible, expand voting rights. He filed lawsuits against the more blatant suppression efforts in states and counties.

He also demanded that state legislatures do their part to expand voting rights by lifting the felon bans that bar tens of thousands of mostly black and Hispanic ex-felons from the polls. This is no small point. The five Deep South states, and other old Confederacy states, have been lock down GOP states. However, the increased number of black and Hispanics in these states posed a mortal threat to continued GOP dominance in those states. That is if there were no barriers propped up to their registering and voting. The rigid maintenance of the ex-felon ban was the key to the GOP ethnic cleanse of the polls in those vital states.

Sessions was seen by Trump and conservatives as the man to make sure that happened. He was the final step in the GOP plan for permanent national political control. When he had the chance during his tenure as a US Attorney, as state attorney general, and as a U.S. Senator, he cheer-led voter ID laws, relentlessly hunted down and prosecuted every real and imagined voter fraud act, railed against the pre-clearance provision of section 5 of the VRA. And, though he grudgingly voted for an extension of the VRA in 2006, later expressed buyer's remorse about it.

The VRA is the major roadblock to the range of GOP subterfuges to ensure that the bulk of America's voting majority remains its majority. That is white, male conservatives, rural, blue collar voters in the Deep South and Heartland states. These are the voters that put Presidents Reagan, Bush Sr, W. Bush, and now Trump in the White House. They kept failed GOP presidential candidates John Mc Cain and Mitt Romney in the hunt for the Oval Office. Sessions is the absolute key to make sure the GOP maintains its national control if it has its way into perpetuity. Democratic senators sensed the grave peril to voting rights with Sessions running the show at the Justice Department. They voted almost unanimously against his Senate confirmation in January 2017. However, to no avail. They were now a minority in the Senate and could not stop a confirmation.

Scuttling the Voting Rights Act was the centerpiece to that plan. Sessions also had another obsession that posed a dire and frightening peril to blacks and Hispanics. That was drugs. He was the consummate old-line drug warrior.

* * * * *

In March 2017, Attorney General Sessions made it official. The federal government would now reboot its war on drugs. The official word came down in the form of memos from Sessions that ordered federal prosecutors to cease and desist on the soft approach Holder had taken toward prosecuting petty drug offenders. Now prosecutors would demand the harshest sentence, would use the threat to harshly pile on sentence enhancements to browbeat drug offenders into copping a guilty plea, and they would itemize the drugs an offender uses to insure they were slapped with the minimum mandatory sentence.

Sessions wasn't just talking about cracking down on the use of the hard stuff. He had a near paranoid obsession with pot. He railed against its use, called it one of the worst drug evils, and was convinced that it was undermining the nation's morals. Sessions long chomped at the bit to claim the title as America's number one drug warrior. He took giddy delight as a federal prosecutor and a U.S. Attorney in putting the hammer to drug offenders whenever he could. Sessions would likely scoff at the frank admission by disgraced Nixon White House advisor John Ehrlichman. He noted in an interview in *Harpers* in 1994 that the war on drugs was not about law enforcement getting a handle on drug sales and use. It was another weapon to lock up as many blacks as possible.

From its inception in the 1970s, the war on drugs has been a ruthless, relentless, and naked war on minorities, especially African-Americans. Obama and Holder got that. They made it clear that it was time to rethink how the war was being fought and who its prime casualties have been. They pushed hard to get Congress to wipe out a good deal of the blatantly racially skewed harsh drug sentencing for crack versus powder cocaine possession and to eliminate minimum mandatory sentencing. Congress didn't finish the job. As long as Sessions was in the driver's seat at the Justice Department, it wouldn't. The Obama and Holder reforms in low level drug prosecutions did produce positive and dramatic results. The number of minimum mandatory sentences imposed plunged, and there was much more reliance on drug counseling and diversion programs for petty offenders.

With Sessions that would be a thing of the past. Even though countless surveys have found that whites and blacks use drugs in about the same rate, more than 70 percent of those prosecuted in federal courts for drug possession and sale (mostly small amounts of crack cocaine) and given stiff mandatory sentences are blacks. Most those who deal and use crack cocaine aren't violent prone gang members, but poor and increasingly female young blacks. They clearly need treatment not long prison stretches. Obama and Holder understood that.

The federal government's war on drugs before Obama and Holder, and now reignited under Sessions, targeted blacks for a good reason. The top-heavy drug use by young whites—and the crime and violence that go with it—has never stirred any public outcry for mass arrests, prosecutions, and tough prison sentences for white drug dealers, many of whom deal drugs that are directly linked to serious crime and violence. Whites unlucky enough to get popped for drug possession are treated with compassion, prayer sessions, expensive psychiatric counseling, treatment and rehab programs, and drug diversion programs.

Trump highlighted the glaring racial double standard in how the drug crisis is dealt with by law enforcement, the media, and elected officials when the prime offenders are white. In March 2017, he signed an executive order establishing a commission charged with making recommendations on dealing with the opioid crisis. At the signing, the talk by Trump and other administration officials was about a big ramp up in treatment, counseling, addiction recovery programs, and health services to alleviate the crisis. Even the term politicians and the media use to describe it, "epidemic," suggests that it's an illness, a sickness, a condition, but not a criminal offense. There was not one word from Trump or White House officials about more arrests, tougher sentencing and incarceration for offenders.

Trump appointed his close political backer, New Jersey Governor Chris Christie to head up the commission that would come back with the recommendations on dealing with the crisis. Christie made plain what the focus would be on, "What we need to come to grips with is addiction is a disease and no life is disposable. We can help people by giving them appropriate treatment. This was in sharp contrast to Sessions' tough stance on drug crimes which he saw as solved by more convictions and jail time. Then again Sessions wasn't talking about white addicts, the ones whom the opioid crisis affected the most. However, Trump was. That was evident with his March White House conference and executive order establishing a commission on the Opioid "epidemic" that he was talking about addicts that were likely not in inner cities but rural and suburban areas. That is those in Trump friendly voting areas.

A frank admission that the drug laws are biased and unfair and have not done much to combat the drug plague, would be an admission of failure. It could ignite a real soul-searching over whether all the billions of dollars that have been squandered in the failed and flawed drug war—the lives ruined by it, and the families torn apart by the rigid and unequal enforcement of the laws—has really accomplished anything.

This might call into question why people use and abuse drugs in the first place—and if it is really the government's business to turn the legal screws on some drug users while turning a blind eye to others?

The greatest fallout from the nation's failed drug policy is that it has further embedded the widespread notion that the drug problem is exclusively a black problem. This makes it easy for on-the-make politicians to grab votes, garner press attention, and balloon state prison budgets to jail more black offenders, while continuing to feed the illusion that we are winning the drug war.

Sessions saw it differently. In his fundamentalist, self-righteous, puritanical world, drug users were the scourge of the nation. They must be swiftly and mercilessly removed from the streets, workplaces, schools, and any other place that their presence subverts the good upstanding morals of the nation. Sessions said as much in a memo when he claimed that his tough drug crackdown will "advance public safety, and promote respect for our legal system." It would do neither. It would balloon prison building, the hiring and maintaining of waves of corrections officers, and further bloat state budgets. Worst of all it would do what it was always intended to do, and that's be a war on minorities and especially blacks by jamming countless more numbers of them back in America's prisons, and gutting education, housing and job spending programs, and vital health services in the process. In short, the very support programs that have proven to be the best antidote to reducing crime.

There was yet another issue that months before Sessions took the helm at the Justice Department had become a crisis issue and had become both a source of national racial polarization. That was the perennial issue of police killings of young black men and, in turn, the slaying of police officers in Baton Rouge, Dallas, and other cities. Trump made it clear just who he blamed for the violence

*   *   *   *   *

"They certainly have ignited people and you see that ... It's a very, very serious situation and we just can't let it happen." The "they," he told then *Fox News* Host Bill O'Reilly, was Black Lives Matter, the activist group that captured Trump and media's attention in June 2016 following the police slayings of young blacks in several cities. Trump went even further and called them a grave threat to police and left little doubt that they, not abusive police departments, would be his target if elected. Trump left no doubt as to just who he expected to do the targeting, "We are going to have to, perhaps, talk to the attorney general about it or do something."

Sessions got the message on just what Trump expected. In April 2017, he made public a terse two-page memo in which he bluntly stated that the carefully crafted consent decrees that Holder had worked out with several troubled police departments such as the one in Ferguson, Missouri, following the turmoil that followed the slaying of Michael Brown, would either be scrapped, or failing that, virtually ignored. In polite bureaucratic parlance, he said the policy would be "reviewed." The Justice Department, then, for all practical purposes would be out of the business of brokering any new consent decrees to curb police abuse with other troubled police departments. Sessions echoed his boss, Trump, in explaining his rationale for getting out of the business of police reform:

"The Attorney General and the new leadership in the Department are actively developing strategies to support the thousands of law enforcement agencies across the country that seek to prevent crime and protect the public,"

This was a major blow to the diligent effort that Holder and former President Obama had made to rein in police misconduct in major cities. A year after Obama took office in 2009, the Justice Department had opened 25 investigations into law enforcement agencies and either brokered or enforced 14 consent decrees, and some other agreements that spelled out what measures police departments were expected to take to reduce conflict with minority communities.

Trump and Sessions reversal was more than a repudiation of the efforts that Obama's Justice Department had made to curb police violence. It sent the deliberate signal to police officials that they would no longer be subject to any scrutiny worth much by the Justice

Department. In short, they had a staunch friend, not a perceived antagonist, at the department.

Police union officials wasted no time in hailing the move as tantamount to taking the wraps off police departments when it came to fighting crime; up to and including whatever use of deadly force police officers deemed necessary to get the job done. If that meant more stop and frisk stops, searches and arrests that stepped over the Constitutional line and outrageously infringed on individual rights then so be it. The ends justified the means and the means in Sessions' eyes always would be in the hands of the police to use however they deemed appropriate.

The blind eye to police abuse, scrapping voting rights protections, igniting the resurgence in the drug wars, all added up to a draconian sea change in how the Justice Department would operate with Sessions running the show. The Justice Department would no longer be the one federal agency that minorities for a half century since the civil rights era of the 1960s had looked to to right civil rights wrongs. If anything, it was now a sworn foe. It was a department that would wear the label not of a justice department, but an injustice department.

CHAPTER 4

Three, Four More Scalia's on the High Court

At a campaign rally in August 2016 in Pennsylvania, GOP presidential nominee Trump didn't hesitate when asked the kind of judges he'd like to see on the high court. "I will pick great Supreme Court justices like Antonin Scalia." He repeated that pledge in his acceptance speech at the Republican National Convention in July.

This was not simply a double down on his praise of Scalia as the judge who, along with Clarence Thomas, was at the top of his High Court heroes list. He signaled that his picks would not just be garden variety strict constructionists, but activists and influencers on the bench. They would be judges who wouldn't just base their rulings on the standard conservative legal doctrine. They would cajole, hector and badger other judges to toe the hard-conservative line in their rulings. Judges who would have the gall, when it suited their purpose, to not even try and hide their political partisanship.

Scalia was the textbook example of this kind of judge. He didn't even try to provide a constitutional cover for his court push to give

Florida to Bush in the 2000 presidential election. As he famously and shamelessly said then, "The only issue was whether we should put an end to it, after three weeks of looking like a fool in the eyes of the world."

Scalia fully played the part of the pugnacious partisan ultra-conservative judge. Nowhere was that on more stunning display than for the two decades that he served as the court schoolmaster to Thomas. Along the way, he ensured that the other justices looked hard over their shoulders at him when they huddled to craft an opinion in a case. It was no accident that after Scalia's death in February 2016, it looked and even sounded like an almost moderate court on some of its rulings: on abortion rights, affirmative action, voting rights and the feds paying for contraceptives at religious hospitals. The outcome would have almost certainly been different if Scalia had been there.

GOP Vice Presidential contender Mike Pence made the Trump-Scalia axis official when he vowed to a campaign crowd in July 2016 in Michigan that Trump's High Court pick would hit the bench with the practically sworn duty to slam down the curtain on *Roe v. Wade*. This was tantamount to promising to say, to heck with law, prior rulings or deliberations, the judge would just knock out abortion rights period. Pence didn't stop there. He repeatedly tossed out the mantra that Trump would appoint strict constructionists in his court appointments, and not just for a Scalia-type judicial hit on abortion rights. This was a prime advertisement for unapologetic conservative judicial activism in the cookie-cutter mold of a Scalia.

Trump didn't publicly drop Scalia's name at every turn solely because he considered him the judge with the right stuff. He was the one person that he knew, above all others, was considered a demigod among party ultra-conservatives, pro-lifers, and evangelicals.

In decades past, many Democratic and Republican-appointed

justices scrapped party loyalties and based their legal decisions solely on the merit of the law, constitutional principles, and the public good. Scalia was a judicial horse of a different color. The tip-off that judges like him would vote their ideology rather than the law came from George W. Bush. On the presidential campaign trail in 2000, Bush was asked if elected what kind of judge he'd look for and nominate. He didn't hesitate.

He pledged to appoint "strict constructionists" to the court and specifically named Thomas, Scalia, and William Rehnquist as the judges who perfectly typified that description. By then the three had already carved out a hard-line niche as three of the most reflexive, knee-jerk, reactionary jurists to grace the court in decades. Their votes to torpedo, water down, eviscerate or erode rights on all issues from abortion to civil rights were so predictable they could have been mailed in.

A Supreme Court judge can sit on the court for years even de-cades and watch as legions of Republicans and Democrats come and go in Congress and the White House. Scalia certainly did. All the while, they shape and remake law and public policy for future years with their votes, rulings and opinions. Trump knew that a few more Scalias on the bench would ensure that the High Court did just that, and his way.

* * * * *

The importance the hard right put in an ideologically compliant Supreme Court to do its legal bidding was never more in evidence when a conservative majority on the court waged virtual war against the Obama administration. Thomas provided the opening hint of things to come in that war.

In a *C-SPAN* Interview in April 2013, he was asked pointedly his thoughts about President Obama. The characteristically terse and guarded Thomas simply said, "I shook hands with him at the inauguration to be polite but I've had no in-depth conversation." He did not elaborate. There was no need. He made it clear that any interaction with Obama was solely "to be polite." Thomas along with the four other justices had virtually turned the number 5 to 4 into a fine art. That was the reflexive vote of the five high court judges against any and every Obama administration position, initiative, or piece of legislation that was under legal fire and that wound up before the court.

The much talked about Hobby Lobby ruling in June 2014, which the five held that privately-held corporations could refuse on religious grounds to cover the cost of contraceptives for its employees was typical. It was a blow to Obama's Affordable Care Act. It gave more power to corporations, and opened the floodgates wide to using religion to scuttle anything corporations didn't like. The ruling was the standard template for the five justices' war on Obama. The five ruled more than a dozen times at various times that Obama had allegedly badly abused his constitutional authority in decisions, appointments, and court appeals. Their rulings had little to do with executive abuse since many of the cases were routine appeals. They simply undergirded the GOP's shrill war hoop that Obama was a serial constitutional usurper.

That was just a warm up drill in the court's war on Obama. The heavy-duty stuff was the court majority's rulings on the big-ticket issues of voting rights, affirmative action, corporate and property rights, and union and environmental protections. The court ruled against him in more than 60 percent of these cases. In more than a dozen cases in a two-year span during his White House tenure the vote against him was 5 to 4.

Past presidents have generally gotten most of what they want from the high court. According to Adam Winkler, UCLA constitutional law professor, on average presidents have won about 70 percent of the cases the court's decided that their administration backed. Obama was not even close to that number.

The GOP's relentless judicial war against Obama was on its greatest display when Obama nominated Appeals court judge Merrick Garland to fill the vacant seat of Scalia. Virtually moments after Obama made the announcement, Senate Majority leader Mitch McConnell made it plain that the nomination was DOA. There would be no hearings, no votes, and absolutely no action by the Senate on Garland. He was as good as his word. By September 2016, Garland had passed the 170-day mark with his nomination on hold. With that he gained the dubious distinction of smashing the all-time record for a Supreme Court nominee getting no action on his appointment by the Senate. McConnel justified the freeze out of Garland with the pithy retort that a court appointment should be the purview of the next President. He really meant the next GOP President, or so he hoped in his play for time.

Thomas tipped his and the other four's hand when he attributed his inauguration hand shake with Obama solely to politeness. Yet, he and the other four were anything but polite in their determined assault on him. Their assault had little to do with the law, and everything to do with politics and ideology. Their decisions against him were blatant partisan political pandering. Thomas and the other four justices were appointed by Republican presidents. The other four justices that almost always backed the Obama administration in their votes on court cases were appointed by him or former president, Bill Clinton.

Thomas took that even further and was the court's first openly public recluse. He refused to utter a peep during any of the oral arguments before the court for more than two decades on the bench. But then there was not much need since his anti-Obama votes were already guaranteed. The rare times that Obama won victories were much less than met the eye. In the court's ruling that invalidated the Defense of Marriage Act and in declining to rule on the California's Proposition 8 voter approved ban on gay marriage, in June 2013, the rulings were on the narrowest of grounds and in both cases, there was no mention of the constitutionality or not of same sex marriage. Even then the wins were narrow. Thomas and three of the reflexive anti-Obama conservatives voted to uphold DOMA. He and two of the others voted in the minority to uphold Prop 8.

The Supreme Court ended nearly every other session after Obama took office in 2009 by taking every opportunity to escalate its war on him. It was a war the court would have waged without end against him and any other moderate Democrat that sat in the White House. Trump was keenly attuned to that.

* * * * *

The other indication that Trump would appoint judge's hostile to civil rights was the list of nearly a dozen names of his potential court picks he got with lots of help from the ultra-conservative Heritage Foundation. He made their names public in May 2016. He added a few more names in September that included a woman, a Hispanic, Asian, and an African-American judge. But that was mostly for cosmetic and public relations purposes. Those on the original list were almost all white males, and hard line opponents of abortion, same-sex marriage, voting rights expansion, and increased federal regulations. The names that he added as a sop to diversity were cut from the same cloth as those on his first list.

Trump's picks would be judges exactly in the mold of Scalia

and Thomas. Said Trump," This list is definitive and I will choose only from it in picking future justices of the United States Supreme Court." The stakes were enormous this time around. Trump almost certainly would have the chance to pick one maybe two more justices during his term replacing the two-aging liberal and a moderate judge on the court

The right plainly wanted more judges on the bench who would rigidly toe the ultra-conservative line. The court became even more important as a political tool for the conservative remake of the country when it became clear that just having more conservatives in the Senate and the House was not enough to roll back the gains in civil, women's and labor rights of the past half century. Democrats even as the minority in Congress could obstruct or outright kill legislation through the filibuster or other delay tactics. And with the nation's population and voter demographics rapidly changing with more minorities, women, same sex, and youth, who were mostly Democrats, and implacably hostile to conservative positions, this could put more spine in Democrats to stand firm against the machinations of conservatives in Congress, and especially those of the Trump administration.

The right correctly saw the Supreme Court not just as a neutral arbiter to settle legal disputes. It was a lethal weapon to skirt congressional gridlock and serve a dual role as a judicial and legislative body. This entailed doing away with the long-standing tradition on the court where justices based their legal decisions solely on the merit of the law, constitutional principles and the public good, and not ideology. Trump and his hard-right conservative backers were fully aware that the court's power to be de facto legislators could last for decades. After all presidents and congresspersons come and go, but justices can sit there until death if they choose. Scalia and Thomas were proof of that. Scalia sat for 30 years and Thomas has sat on the bench for a quarter century.

* * * * *

It didn't take long for Trump to make good on his Scalia clone high court pick. In fact, the judge he would pick as Scalia's replacement came complete with pictures of him and Scalia in warm companionship on a fishing trip in Colorado a year before Scalia's death. Afterwards, Federal Appeals Court Judge, Neil Gorsuch, said he could barely get down a ski run in Colorado because he was so blinded by tears on news of Scalia's death. This was not a private utterance or personal feeling of deep emotion that he shared with friends and family. He told of his profound sorrow in a speech in April 2016 at Case Western University. Gorsuch wanted the world to know that Scalia was more than just a heartfelt friend. He was a man, and a judge, whose legal and judicial ideas he was in total lockstep with. Gorsuch also had another judge who he much admired That judge was Thomas.

The two hints were first, Gorsuch's own words, "I am blown away by Thomas's dissent," The dissent in question was a case involving the government's use of eminent domain power. Thomas hit the ceiling in roundly condemning it as a violation of the Constitution's prohibition against property. This was a touchy case that irked both liberals, libertarians, and conservatives. To Gorsuch and Thomas, it fit squarely in with their hard read of the Constitution. Or, as Gorsuch put it in applauding Thomas, it violated "the plain textual meaning of the property taking clause of the Constitution."

Thomas and Scalia wrapped themselves in loving embrace in the "originalism" of the Constitution. They saw it as their sworn duty to defend every comma and period of it as the sacred word from on high which could not be violated. With Thomas, it was more. He'd been on a 25-year search and destroy mission to smite down anything that remotely smacked of modern-day, case by case interpretation of its clauses and provisions. Gorsuch plainly liked everything about that.

It was not just their Siamese twin read of the Constitution vis-à-vis modern day thorny public policy and legal issues that typed Gorsuch as every bit as dangerous as Thomas. There was the revealing passage in one of his legal writings in which he protested that a judge should not be a "pragmatic social-welfare maximizer" who makes decisions "only with a radically underdetermined choice to make." Translated, this was a judge who interpreted the law in any manner that remotely could be considered social engineering strays onto dangerous ground.

The ultimate horror on the High Court was not having another judge in the mold of Scalia. But having one in the mold of Thomas. The two would now form a powerful one two punch that would be far more devastating than anything than the Scalia-Thomas combo offered.

*   *   *   *   *

Gorsuch certainly had the judicial history to prove that. Between 2007 and 2016, in ten of 14 cases involving discrimination, he shot down all union and employee litigant arguments charging discrimination in back pay, hiring, and termination cases. In a case in 2012, involving pay and an employee termination, he made clear that the burden to prove discrimination is always on the petitioner.

He applied his "originalist" read of the law to cases involving trucker rights, safety and health, and the termination of a whistle-blower. In a 2016 case involving an employee suit that charged retaliation, Gorsuch blasted the long-standing standard that permitted indirect evidence of employment discrimination. He noted that the standard had "no useful role to play in First Amendment retaliation cases." He didn't stop there. Even more ominously, he noted that the standard may have no application in Title VII discrimination cases "because of the confusion and complexities its application can invite."

In separate sex, race, and disability discrimination cases, Gorsuch again put the burden to prove retaliation and discrimination directly on the employee. The requirement to prove intentional discrimination had always been a colossal barrier to winning discrimination cases. This is a near impossibility. Corporations and government agencies faced with racial, gender, disability, and labor equity discrimination suits routinely hid behind this defense.

For nearly a century, discrimination cases have been the most contentious, hotly-debated, and far reaching in shaping and changing law and public policy in America. They have done much to advance civil rights, economic parity, and labor protections for tens of millions of Americans. So, Gorsuch's rulings and dissents were more than academic curiosity. They would have a direct bearing on crucial upcoming cases involving racial and gender discrimination currently before the high court as well as cases that would be before the court in the years to come. The court that Gorsuch sat on would have its share of these cases. A few of the discrimination cases that were already in the SCOTUS pipeline at the time Gorsuch was confirmed demonstrated that.

One would determine how much spending on educational resources school districts must do on students with disabilities. Another was a challenge to school districts on the right of transgender students to use and have school restrooms that conform to their gender identity. Another case dealt with the perennial question of whether the government must grant religious schools public funding for materials for the classroom and playgrounds.

There was also a slew of patent rights, property right, eminent domain, and zoning cases that could give even greater power to corporations to call the shots in its dealing with employees, consumers and litigants. They could also even further reduce the ability of aggrieved consumers and employees, many of whom were minorities, to bring class action lawsuits.

There were two other crucial issues that the court had let tenuously dangle. One was voting rights. The high court in 2013 struck down Section 5 of the 1965 Voting Rights Act. It required states mostly in the Deep South and West that had long and outrageous histories of using every gimmick to disenfranchise blacks, Hispanics, and Native Americans to get pre-clearance from the Justice Department before making any changes in its election laws. There was still the law's Section 2. This forbade any "denial or abridgment of the right of any citizen of the United States to vote on account of race or membership in a language-minority group." Suits could still be filed to stop states from voter suppression ploys. If, but more likely when, this was challenged, Gorsuch's hard line "originalist" read of the Constitution would likely regard this Section as an impediment to state's rights to decide its voting laws and procedures.

The other issue was affirmative action. The laws and policies backing tightly constrained affirmative action measures on campuses and in public agencies are still in place. Conservatives have been relentless in tossing up lawsuits at every turn to obliterate anything that reaffirmed affirmative action. They suffered a narrow setback in 2016 when the High Court upheld the University of Texas's affirmative action program. This would not be the end of the issue. There would be another challenge at some point. An indication on just how

Gorsuch could rule came from Thomas's one-page dissent in the Texas case in which he flatly said that affirmative action is "categorically prohibited."

Trump's Scalia-cloned High Court could render horrific decisions on cases that would turn the clock back on civil rights, labor protections and employee discrimination for decades to come. This was exactly what Trump had in mind when he brashly and repeatedly said he'd do everything possible to put more Scalias on the Supreme Court. Gorsuch was the first in his effort to make good on that pledge.

CHAPTER 5

For Sale:
Education and Housing

In February 2017, Trump had a prized photo-op session in the Oval Office with a pleasantly smiling contingent of presidents and administrators of Historically Black Colleges and Universities. Trump gave the clear impression from the photo-op that he'd go out of his way to boost funding and support for HBCU's. It didn't take long to shatter that delusion. Days after the meeting with the college presidents, Trump signed an executive order moving the Initiative on Historically Black Colleges and Universities from the Department of Education into the executive office of the White House. In other words, into his hands. HBCUs would, in effect, be at his mercy.

If he liked a particular HBCU, and its president, and that meant toeing the Trump line on education policy, then the favored college president would likely find that his campus would be among the select few in Trump's politicized world.

In case anyone didn't get the message of where Trump might go with his HBCU plaything. In April 2017, he signed a stop gap trillion-dollar budget measure. In his remarks at the signing, he made a veiled threat to take a hard look at the Historically Black College and University Capital Financing Program. Trump seemed to think that singling out Black Colleges for special funding might be a race based measure that he and conservatives have waged a two decade long ruthless war to wipe all vestiges of off the landscape.

The howl from civil rights leaders and House Democrats was swift. They rightly noted that Trump ignorantly misunderstood or deliberately distorted what the funding measure for HBCU's entailed. HBCUs designation as black colleges have nothing to do with a racial designation. It rests solely on their status as colleges and universities, their mission and their accreditation status. Trump quickly walked his crude threat back. He claimed that he had "unwavering" support for black colleges. It didn't change the fact that his shift of oversight over HBCU programs gave him a say so over the affairs of black colleges. Despite his flowery words about making HBCU's his "priority," he didn't make them priority enough to add any more dollars to their funding.

* * * * *

Trump's photo-op go-round with the black college presidents and the seeming diminution of resources and support to their colleges, brought into view how his controversial Education Secretary, Betsy DeVos was widely perceived by blacks and the reason for their negative perception. It was her mission to sell the Trump line and agenda on education which, put simply, was to swing the wrecking ball even harder and faster on public education. Her avowed mission was to shove every federal dollar she could to fulfill the conservative's happy dream of dumping public schools for vouchers and school choice.

DeVos was the perfect choice for that. Her long running war on public schools was well known. She bankrolled and chaired school choice lobbying groups, poured millions of dollars into a national propaganda effort to sell school choice, and backed a failed referendum on the ballot in Michigan in 2000 to siphon massive amounts of public school dollars to private and religious schools. It was voted down. At every turn, though, she greased the skids for her rich cronies to open charter schools on the taxpayer dime.

The ones hurt the most by this are low income black students in the already chronically cash-strapped, underserved urban school districts where charters have wildly proliferated. The vicious cycle is virtually the same in all of these public-school districts. Students exodus a local public school, the revenue short-fall for the school gets even shorter, school programs and services are cut. In desperation, parents then flee the schools in droves for a local charter. The charters get more students and in turn, soak up more public revenue, while the district's public schools lose even more money. That results in even more cuts, with the educational bar for the public schools dropping even lower.

Trump, DeVos, and free market educators, applaud this and are determined to do everything they could to provide more dollars to these schools, while cash starving public schools to the point they literally go out of business. The glaring problem beyond hammering the neediest students is that there's much evidence that charter schools in many cases are no better than public schools in insuring black students get a better education. Studies especially are mixed on charter versus public school performance in urban districts. In some charters, students did improve their test scores. However, in many others they didn't. The bigger problem with this mixed report card further raises the question, why, then the massive push to cash starve public schools to create more of charter schools that may or may not work?

* * * * *

This question, and the issue of the role of public education, lurked underneath the concerns black college presidents had with Trump and DeVos. For her part, DeVos tried mightily to make nice with some of the HBCU heads who she and Trump believed would play along with their scheme to totally gut public education. The return for the black college head who goes along with it was to have a sliver more access to Trump, and possibly get a few more dollars deposited in their school's coffers.

DeVos, however, got a rude shock in May 2017. She was invited to give the commencement address at Bethune-Cookman University. The invitation conformed nicely with Trump school privatization plan. The college was a legendary Historically Black College that relied on a mix of public and private funding. What didn't fit was the reaction of the students. When they refused to act like cheerful, plastic marionettes and clap and cheer for her on cue, the visibly flustered Bethune-Cookman President saber rattled the students by threatening to mail their degrees to them. This was not just a university president who was piqued at the supposed bad behavior of the students toward an invited guest speaker.

The embarrassment of having Trump's education emissary roundly booed potentially could have had a bad consequence for the university; namely the danger of Bethune-Cookman, and its president, falling off Trump's most pliable black college list. The students simply did what colleges repeatedly pay lip service to, and that's encourage their students to think critically, be active and engaged in their community, and to be the committed leaders of tomorrow. They more than fulfilled that admonition when they made it clear by their negative reaction to DeVos.

DeVos had already experienced the wrath of public school administrators at a couple of other schools that she tried to visit in the weeks immediately after she took office. The administrators, teachers, and public-school officials, particularly those that served mostly black and Hispanic students and were the most financially hard pressed, realized they'd be in the fight for their financial and school program lives with DeVos and Trump. The education budget he unveiled for 2018 in May 2017 left no doubt who would get what at the schools. Charters got tens of millions more dollars in proposed funding which was a 50 percent increase. That wasn't all. He and DeVos openly called for something that has never happened in the history of federal funding of public schools in the country. That's a federal tax credit program at the federal level such as exists in Florida and some other states. This would directly put taxpayers on the hook for bankrolling private schools. This was the ultimate in making the case that education would literally be for sale with the seller being the White House.

∗ ∗ ∗ ∗ ∗

DeVos wasn't the only free market guru who would put a for sale sign on a government agency and mortgage public resources to the highest bidder. There was also now a doctor in the Trump political house who had similar ideas when it came to running another government agency. The agency was HUD.

Former neurosurgeon and black conservative icon, Ben Carson, at first shrugged off any desire to take over the reins of HUD when Trump first broached the idea of appointing him to the post in December 2016. He emphatically declared that he had no government experience that would qualify him to run a federal agency. Most took this to mean that he would quietly recede, if not fade, from public attention. That wasn't to be. Trump saw to that when he brushed aside Carson's momentary candid admission and submitted his name as the Secretary to be of HUD. This was a remarkable but not surprising return from the political dead for Carson.

HUD now would be run by a man who self-admitted that he had no government experience in running a crucial agency that ladles out billions annually in public housing subsidies, rental assistance, and housing finance activities, employs more than 8000 workers and administrators and operates more than 100 subsidy programs. If that's wasn't bad enough, Carson didn't even like what HUD did. He had a long and well-documented track record of lambasting housing discrimination suits, over-dependence on "social safety net" programs, getting government out of competition with private enterprise, and denouncing anything that supposedly deadened individual initiative.

This was the stuff of snickers, chuckles, and lampooning when Carson was simply private citizen Carson, or, the mercifully brief, failed GOP presidential candidate Carson. Few then could ever imagine that he would ever be in a position to actually act on any of his rabid, and antique ultra-right notions of how a government should be run. However, with the Trump HUD post offering, Carson now could give free rein to his basest impulses about privatizing public housing.

HUD has been a long standing favorite whipping boy of ultra-conservatives. They have repeatedly ripped HUD for its alleged corruption and cronyism, and complained long and loud about the high cost and waste of public housing projects and vouchers for low income renters. However, HUD's biggest sin to them has been that it supposedly shackles private housing developers by putting the federal government directly in the business of subsidizing home ownership. They don't stop here. They have long made the totally unsupported and outlandish claim that HUD's butting into the housing business was one of the biggest reasons for the 2008 financial meltdown.

* * * * *

The only thing missing from the conservative hit plan on HUD was finding the right someone to do the dirty work to totally defrock the agency. And who better than Carson? He is black, and he and other conservatives never tire of repeating his woeful tale of rising from the hard scrabble streets of an urban ghetto to the pinnacle of success in the medical profession. He even lightly played on it again when he said with hopefully his tongue deep in his cheek that he had great expertise on poor people living in public housing because he once lived in a ghetto.

This didn't seem to be much of a consideration for Carson when he appeared before a Senate Subcommittee panel in June 2017 to back his boss's plan to totally erase from the HUD books the Community Development Block Grant Program. The program has been a lifeline for local governments since the 1970s to patch up crumbling housing, provide housing subsidies, and food and care for the homeless, the majority of whom are low income persons in urban areas. Carson gave the standard conservative argument for gutting or eliminating programs that serve the poor. That was that they were wasteful and squandered taxpayer dollars on frivolous, non-essential frills.

There wasn't much chance that Congress would totally eliminate the program. There were just too many GOP represented districts that also got a lot of the block grant money to improve their housing stock. However, Carson's push for doing away with the program was another hint that public funding and programs that HUD had anything to do with would be in for rough sledding.

Carson punctuated that when he told the Senate Subcommittee that the budget had "been forced on us." That raised Senate eyebrows trying to figure out how a major federal agency could have its arms twisted to receive its funding. However, Carson's real point was not the money but the agency, or rather, its stated mandate." If it was up to him, he said, he'd quickly change that and go after seed money for investors and private groups.Bottom of Form

The trotting out of Carson to deliver the right-wing gospel from on high in the hacking up of HUD was part of another by now familiar tact used by ultra-conservatives during the Obama years. That was to propose Carson as a GOP presidential contender. It worked twice in 2012 and 2016. His "candidacy" quickly fizzled out both times. However, Carson didn't go away. He resolutely backed Trump's presidential bid every media chance he got and Trump didn't forget. HUD was his reward.

Carson was the perfect cover for Trump to try and wreck a federal agency. He was widely admired for his personal saga of a black who pulled himself by his bootstrap through his own initiative. This aura of supposed personal triumph served him well during his confirmation hearing for the HUD post. Democrats on the Senate hearing committee handled him with kid gloves. Even committee member Massachusetts senator Elizabeth Warren. One of the Senate's fiercest consumer advocate and populist, pulled her punches in questioning Carson, and ultimately voted to confirm him. The thought of going to hard after a black man, just wouldn't sit well publicly. So Carson was home free.

As such he could do as much damage as conservatives wanted to do to HUD with hopefully minimal attention to it. The damage in this case would be wreaked by a black HUD Secretary who believed and stated that "poverty is a state of mind."

CHAPTER 6

The Never-Ending War on Obamacare

In an interview on *60 minutes* in September 2015, GOP presidential candidate Trump, boldly told the nation that once in the White House he'd get rid of the Affordable Care Act. He claimed that he had a plan that would provide cheap insurance for every American. In the months after, whenever the subject came up in interviews, rallies, and candidate debates, Trump would immediately chant "repeal and replace" Obamacare.

Trump was very much a Johnny come lately to the anti-Obamacare fight. The GOP had already been at the assault Obamacare campaign for a long, long time.

The GOP-controlled House Ways and Means in October 2015 was the first of the three GOP congressional committees "investigating" Obamacare to try and pulverize it—again. GOP committee members pounded hard on the stock GOP hit points; it was a mess because of a lousy computer system, thousands had gotten sticker shock after getting cancellation notices, there were big sneaky insurance price hikes on the way. Then there were the subsidies that were too costly and for the most part weren't even available to the middle-class. The capper was that then President Obama supposedly blatantly lied when he promised no one would lose their current health insurance plan due to Obamacare.

The GOP hit points were based on the usual mix of lies, half-truths, and wild distortions. Thousands had by then signed up in fact for various health plans both online and through the state exchanges. The vast majority of policy holders had either workplace plans and grandfathered polices that were purchased before March 2010. They were not forced at Obamacare gunpoint to switch to costly coverage plans. The penalties for not having insurance that were supposed to be financial killers amounted to a $95 fine or 1 percent of an individual's income, whichever was greater.

The subsidies to help pay for coverage were bankrolled to the tune of more than a half trillion dollars. This would slash the actual costs of the various plans offered on the exchanges by more than half for a family of four. Most of those who fell below the poverty line wouldn't be affected by any of this since they'd be covered through expanded Medicaid coverage in most states that's paid for by the federal government. Despite the bluster from some GOP governors about rejecting the Medicaid funding increases, the almost certain rise in health care costs would force states to pay even more for medical coverage to low income persons. Without it the pressure would be great for the hard ball GOP governors to rethink their opposition to taking the beefed-up Medicaid bailout.

Then there were the supposed big price hikes that Obamacare supposedly would trigger. Insurance premium costs would likely jump no matter whether Obamacare existed or not. That was due to inflated medical treatment costs, the impotence of most state regulatory agencies to halt rapacious insurer rate hikes, and the hard reality that programs that emphasize prevention which have proven far more effective in reining in medical costs are still poor step children to the pricey and vastly more profitable drug and surgical treatments that remain the bread and butter staple of the medical establishment.

*   *   *   *   *

Trump and the avowed GOP enemies of Obamacare would never dare publicly say or intimate what many had repeatedly pointed out before, during, and after their warfare against the Act. It was that the group that had been one of the greatest beneficiaries of the Affordable Care Act was African-Americans. The verdict was in even before the first enrollee inked their signature October 1, 2010, on a health care plan under the Affordable Care Act. The law was an unmitigated triumph for the millions of uninsured in America.

The checklist of pluses was well-known. More than 7 million African-Americans now had access to a health plan, there would be subsidies for low-income persons to offset the costs, a half million children would be covered under their parent's plans, millions of dollars would be allocated for research and testing, the establishment of more than 1000 new health care facilities in many rural and urban communities, the National Health Service Corps workforce would be tripled and more than 4 million elderly and disabled African-Americans covered under Medicare would have no cost access to health care preventive services. The triumph was even greater because of the grim figures on the health care crisis that had been a national disgrace for so long for African-Americans

The dismal figures repeatedly told why. Blacks made up a disproportionate number of the estimated 50 million Americans with absolutely no access to affordable or any health care. The majority of black uninsured were far more likely than the one in four whites who were uninsured to experience problems getting treatment at a hospital or clinic. This has had devastating health and public policy consequence. According to major studies, blacks were far more likely than whites to suffer higher rates of catastrophic illness and disease, and were much less likely to obtain basic drugs, tests, preventive screenings, and surgeries. They were more likely to recover slower from illness, and they die much younger.

Studies found that when blacks do receive treatment, the care they receive is more likely to be substandard to that of whites. Reports indicate that even when blacks were enrolled in high quality health plans, the racial gap in the care and quality of medical treatment still remained low. Meanwhile, private insurers routinely cherry picked the healthiest and most financially secure patients in order to bloat profits and hold down costs. American medical providers spent twice as much per patient than providers in countries with universal health care, and they provided lower quality for the grossly inflated dollars. Patients paid more in higher insurance premiums, co-payments, fees, and other hidden health costs.

It was a perfect mix of politics, race, and ignorance and fear that drove Trump and the GOP's mania to dump Obamacare. It included every slander, lie, and false flag, countless votes and threats to defund the Act and a crude attempt at blackmail to shut down the whole government over it. Some claimed that this was big government intrusiveness since it allegedly whipsawed Americans into buying insurance and that it was too costly, too overburdening on businesses, and supposedly too unpopular with a majority of Americans.

The race part was two-fold. One it was proposed by then President Obama. Anything program or initiative that was proposed by him during his eight years in the White House was the trigger for GOP knee jerk opposition. The other part was the great fear of GOP health care reform opponents and the health care industry lobby which includes private insurers, and for a time pharmaceuticals and major medical practitioners was that they'd have to treat millions of uninsured, unprofitable, largely unhealthy blacks. That would be a direct threat to their massive profits. The pharmaceuticals eventually dropped their opposition only after getting assurances that they would not have to cut costs of drugs to make way for more generics and drug competition from Canada and that the millions of newly insured recipients would be drug purchasers.

* * * * *

Trump and the GOP hit plan on Obamacare was always much more than a battle to scrap a health care plan that was supposedly flawed, failed, and a big government intrusion into the lives of Americans. It was a crude and cynical political ploy to inflame millions of Americans and stir hostility to Obama and the Democrats. The GOP banked that its steady attack would give it the political edge to win the House in 2010 and the Senate and the White House in 2016

Even as polls consistently showed that while many Americans had deep concerns and even legitimate fears about the short-term effect of Obamacare, Trump and the GOP continued to bull ahead with its relentless war to do away with it.

Trump's capture of the White House seemingly insured that the final nail would be driven in the coffin for Obamacare. There was a problem though. The GOP either had no concrete plan to replace the ACA or was sharply divided over the myriad of plans that some GOP legislators had proposed.

In January 2017, GOP Kentucky Senator Rand Paul was one of the first to address that complaint. He airily dismissed the prevailing notion that the GOP didn't have any plan to replace the Affordable

Care Act as simply untrue. There were many plans floating around, he claimed, that had been put on the table to replace the law after it was repealed. He was right. There were a lot of proposals that had been floated to replace it after repeal. All of them were equally dreadful.

The GOP had up to that point tossed out as a replacement: scaled down subsidies, tax credits, the expansion of high risk pools, health savings accounts, give insurers the right to peddle insurance in any state they choose, and create Association Health Plans to small businesses and risk pools. The subsidies would scrap the income based measure that Obamacare imposes and substitute instead age as the basis for the subsidy. The subsidy to the poorest and neediest was the linchpin of Obamacare. This made it possible for millions who couldn't afford insurance at any price to purchase it for the first time. To get the tax credits a low wage worker would still have to come up with the cash to purchase insurance. For many that would be problematic.

The high-risk pools supposedly would force thousands of medically indigent persons in pools to insure low cost, access to coverage. It would do just the opposite. The bulk of those in the pool would be the sickest and most in need of continuous medical treatment. They would pay more not less for that coverage. To cover the high cost of maintaining these pools, states would have to pony up more tax dollars or impose premium assessments on insurers who in turn would simply hike their prices to cover the assessments. It would be a continually revolving cost increase cycle with absolutely no guarantee that the sickest and poorest in the pool would get the coverage they need.

The Health Savings Accounts, as with tax credits, would be a bonanza for the rich and high-income persons. They would do nothing for low income persons. They would still have to pay for the high deductibles needed to get insurance at anything that faintly resembles affordable cost. They'd still have to come up with thousands of dollars to salt away in the accounts to pay for the deductibles and to get the tax write offs.

Insurers have long sold insurance wherever they please. However, they had to comply with tough state regulations and consumer protection requirements in some states. Now insurers would simply market their product in states that have the weakest controls and consumer protection standards. There they could charge whatever they want without any pesky interference from state regulators. Even better, they no longer need worry about getting penalized for denying coverage to someone with a pre-existing condition or someone whose treatment would cost tons of money.

This right to pick and choose who an insurer can cover or not was forbidden under Obamacare. However, without Obamacare, and no requirement to cover all, this would mean untold thousands would be out in the health coverage cold again. The Association Health Plans had a catchy and even impressive ring to it. The gaping flaw, though, in the plans is with no tight consumer protection controls in place, insurers in the plan could pick and choose the healthiest ones to provide affordable coverage to while making coverage so expensive for the sickest that it would be prohibitive for them. This would create a two-tier system of health care with the sickest and neediest again out in the cold.

No Obamacare also meant no mandates requiring everyone to have health coverage. The mandate requirement drove the GOP to fits railing that it was a gross violation of individual freedom, and had to go. However, the mandate, the federal subsidies, and the inability of insurers to deny coverage to those with pre-exiting conditions, drove Obamacare. This insured that Americans across the board had to have health coverage. The young, old, the healthy and unhealthy made up the broadest pool for health coverage, and this kept overall costs from skyrocketing. Now with the mandate dumped, insurers would have free rein to charge what they wanted, insure who they wanted, with costs of that coverage continuing to climb.

Three years before Obamacare became law, a staggering 90 million Americans either had no insurance or went without coverage for a period of time during the course of a year or years. Many of them that got coverage also lost that coverage, almost always because they couldn't pay for it, or the insurer dropped them because of a medical condition that the insurer considered too costly to pay for. The state of American health care was worse than abysmal for millions. This was the point of Obamacare, and why it attained the success it did.

The GOP claim that its replacement plan would do much better than that was a falsehood. Though this largely intact version passed the House in May 2017. The Senate was another matter. Trump didn't care. He blustered and badgered the Senate to move quickly and get a replacement plan on his desk for signature. The Senate would certainly modify the draconian House plan. whatever it came up with, the burning question was how would it affect blacks and minorities? The starting point for answering that is Medicaid. Under Obamacare, tens of thousands of lower income persons and minorities for the first time received health coverage under Medicaid. The GOP would end that. Those tens of thousands would be pared from the coverage rolls. That was only the start of the horror for blacks and the poor. Countless more would also get the boot from the program because the GOP plan would radically slash funding for recipients by rolling federal funding for the program into block grants to the states. It would take no imagination to envision that a state, say Mississippi where the big percent of those who get care through Medicaid are black, could use the block grant money on budget items that had nothing to do with health care.

The subsidies that low income persons get to help pay for their coverage would also be long gone. The premium tax credits to offset payment for health care coverage would not go to the poorest of the poor but the higher income earners. The cruelest part of the GOP plan was that when the dust settled tens of millions would be kicked out entirely from health care plans. There only recourse would be a trip to an overcrowded, underserved emergency ward at a jam-packed county hospital.

Trump made another claim about the possible fate of a vital health care program during the 2016 presidential campaign. He promised that he wouldn't touch Medicare. That almost certainly would go the way of his Medicaid hands-off promise. The two programs are, and have always been seen, as Democratic inspired and backed programs. This has made them conservative whipping boys with the usual storehouse of lies about run-away costs, waste, and heavy handed federal intrusion.

Medicaid is the proving ground to convince the millions that benefit from these foundational federal programs, that they aren't really in their best interests. Trump will try to pound home that there are better alternatives, and that the GOP, not the Democrats, is the party that can provide those alternatives. Trump will try mightily to convince many of his backers who have grave doubts about hacking away programs that have been life-savers to them that his health care plan is best for them. For countless numbers of blacks, Medicaid and Obamacare have been at the top of that list of those life-saving programs. This is the next and most deadly phase of Trump and the GOP's never-ending war on health care for blacks and the poor.

CHAPTER 7

Trump's Obama Obsession

At a GOP presidential candidate's forum in early 2015, then presidential candidate Trump, without a blink said, "I don't know if he loves America." The "he" Trump referred to was, of course, then President Obama. The slap at Obama was at that moment simply the latest in Trump's by then three-year campaign to vilify, impugn, slander, and harass Obama as not only not an American citizen, but as an illegitimate President. Trump's ruthless, near obsessive, vendetta of lies against Obama paid big dividends early on. It got him briefly in the hunt for the GOP presidential nomination in 2012. That made him a political household name. Three years later, in 2015, it got him to the top of the GOP presidential pack and kept him there during the primaries.

So, while Trump no longer uttered the words "show me your birth certificate" in the same breath with President Obama, he no longer had to. Yet, none of Trump's brash, loud mouth, neo-nothing, borderline racist jibes would have worked if it weren't for Obama. Polls repeatedly found that a plurality of GOP voters continued to say and believe that Obama was not an American citizen. And since in their eyes and twisted logic he was not an American citizen, it followed he must be a Muslim. In this case, the number of Republicans who said that was not a plurality, but a solid majority. Trump didn't feed that notion. The birther movement and the companion Obama-was-a-Muslim belief never could or would die among the wide body of GOP voters as long as Obama sat in the White House. From the start, there was a canny, calculated, and politically cynical motive behind birtherism, the religion question, and Obama's supposed foreign loyalties, that Trump eagerly latched onto.

It started the instant that Obama declared his presidential candidacy in February 2007. Take your pick of the conservative attacks on him: He was too black. He was not patriotic enough. He was too liberal, too effete, too untested. He was a Muslim, terrorist fellow traveler, and a closet black radical. The shock of an Obama in the White House was simply too much for many to bear. The attacks only served to elevate his stature and importance to dizzying heights among most blacks. Their pride in his presidency knew no bounds. The stark racial implication of this further fueled resentment of Obama among many bigoted whites.

Obama defied the stereotypical textbook look and definition of what an American president was supposed to look like and be like; namely a wooden image middle-aged, or older, white male. That was just the tip of the iceberg. The real value of the silly Obama fed phony controversies was that it was a convenient and serviceable way to ridicule, undermine, and ultimately attempt to derail his policy initiatives on health care, the economy, and a reasoned foreign policy approach.

* * * * *

Obama then was in a real sense Trump's political meal ticket. When things got dull or there was a momentary rough patch on the campaign trial, Trump had Obama as his ready-made whipping boy. Nothing changed even after Trump won the White House. When Democrats started screaming in the weeks after the election for answers about Trump's relations with Russia and Putin, and with even some GOP leaders feeling the heat and making weak soundings about a probe or two here and there, Trump quickly trotted out his Obama meal ticket. He made the ludicrous claim that Obama wiretapped him during the campaign. He demanded that Congress investigate Obama.

It was tempting to chalk his Obama fixation up to yet another Trump scheme to deflect attention from his Russia connection. In part it was. However, there was more, much more to this.

Trump's persistent use of Obama as his foil wasn't just to slander his presidency. It was to slander him. It wasn't just political, it was personal. The two couldn't be separated. Trump repeatedly made clear during the early stages of his campaign that if he got in the White House he'd sign any and every executive order he could to try and halt, gut, or obliterate every initiative that Obama had ever put in place.

Trump's verbal assault on all of Obama's initiatives normally would have been the end of it. Presidents from an opposing party, to varying degrees, quickly sign executive orders to roll back some of their predecessor's initiatives and actions when they take office. However, Trump's obsessive attacks on Obama had another aim beyond mere personal vindictiveness and deflecting attention from his disastrous administration. It sent the strong signal to his base that he would try and demolish everything that they loathed about Obama; not just his policies, but what he personally stood for.

Obama was an eight-year embarrassment to the chronic Obama

haters. He was liberal. He was a Democratic. And most odious to them, he was black. Tea Party demonstrators greeted Obama at many stops during his first two years in office with placards, signs and pictures that depicted him in the most-lewd, grotesque and often animal-like characterizations. This went way beyond the bounds of normal political attacks and criticism of a president. It was blatantly personal, and showed the depth of the personal distaste many had for Obama and they were not shy about showing it. The Tea Party took much heat during this period for race-baiting. The attacks stung and hit home, and they retooled, repackaged refined their attacks and slogans to the deficit, the budget, spending cuts, and alleged Obama scandals. This was carefully designed to yank the albatross of race off the Tea Party and the GOP's back. That hardly meant, though, that race was off the GOP table as a major political weapon in the GOP's political attack arsenal.

Trump at points during his campaign made no effort to correct or reprimand anyone at his townhalls and rallies who got up and vilified Obama in personal terms. This reinforced the point that Trump would make again and again that Obama was not fit from a political or personal standpoint to occupy the White House. At times during the presidential campaign Trump seemed to be running against Obama, not Hillary Clinton.

Even Trump's very belated acknowledgement in the latter stage of his campaign that Obama was an American citizen was said matter of fact. There was absolutely no elaboration, let alone showing any sign of contrition for waging his ruthless and prolonged campaign to slur him as an alien.

Trump set the template early in his presidential quest about how to go after Obama. That was to pithily toss out a sensational, outrageous accusation against or about him without a shred of evidence to back it up and then sit back and watch the media plaster it out as a headline or top headline news feature. The damage was done and the mission of getting tongues wagging about Obama and get legions believing there must be some truth to it was accomplished.

A month after he officially assumed office in January 2017, he made the eye-popping charge that Obama had wiretapped him during the campaign. He doubled down on that by demanding a Congressional probe into it. The hope was that the more who believed there was truth to the accusation would serve to whittle away yet another tiny chunk from Obama's well-established legacy of personal honor and integrity. This was part and parcel of Trump's strategy to keep the focus on Obama and in the process, deflect any attention from Trump's checkered dealings.

The wiretap accusation quickly fell flat because it was another Trump lie. This was less important than making the accusation, and getting the media and public headline hit on Obama. This wouldn't be the end. Trump would never rest until he'd destroyed Obama's political legacy, and Obama as well.

* * * * *

Now with the presidency safely tucked away, Trump could add some teeth to his threat to do away with Obama's legacy. He had continually vowed that when that day came he would go after what he called then-President Obama's executive orders. Or, as he crudely put it, his "illegal and overreaching executive orders." He repeatedly came back to that threat on the campaign trail, echoing the standard GOP hit line that Obama supposedly went way overboard and usurped his presidential authority by using his pen to make law. On day one of his swearing in, he wasted no time in doing exactly what he told an interviewer he'd do.

His first act was to sign an executive order nailing the one law above all others that he made a campaign mantra to nail, that is Obamacare. His executive order directed agencies to "waive, defer, grant exemptions" to any part of Obamacare they choose. Getting rid of many of Obama's executive orders wouldn't be so easy. Some were firmly ensconced as law and would require extensive public comment, hearings, and review. It was a long, tedious, drawn-out process. Others had been in place long enough that government agencies had made them part of their compliance requirements.

Nothing drove Trump and GOP leaders to fits of anger faster than Obama's touch of his pen to an executive order. They were hot because he had the power to wield the executive pen in defiance of, and as an end around, every congressional roadblock and obstacle they tossed up to block any and everything that he proposed in his second term. And because his executive orders had the force of law behind them. So, for instance, when there was zero possibility of getting even the faintest, most tepid, gun control measure through Congress, Obama signed a few executive orders that put some peripheral checks on gun sales. In all, Obama, signed a couple hundred orders.

That was more than enough for the GOP to threaten to file lawsuits and even drop loud hints that his actions may even warrant impeachment.

* * * * *

The GOP's hysterical ire at Obama wasn't lost on Trump. There was absolutely no doubt that he'd move with breakneck speed to hit back, and hit back hard, at Obama by going after his executive orders.

Conservative advocacy groups and GOP leaders had a dizzying array of Obama's executive orders that they demanded he immediately wipe off the books. Clean power plant regulations, transgender bathrooms, overtime pay for federal contracted work, immigration restrictions easing, and the gun control orders were high on their hit list. In fact, every single one of Obama's executive orders had been listed, checked off, and targeted for "review" by Trump. Some would survive, and some others wouldn't. Those that would be eliminated would be in key vital public policy areas that provided protections for blacks and minorities. They would include measures such as gun control, environmental, immigration, and workplace controls that were slated to become ancient history.

Despite the GOP's rage at Obama for wielding his executive pen, the truth was that he was near the bottom on the list of presidents in the number of executive orders issued. The last president who issued orders at a lower rate than Obama was Grover Cleveland. GOP Presidents Reagan and George W. Bush issued far more executive orders per day in office than Obama. It was not really the number or rate of executive orders, however, that Obama issued that raised the hackles of the GOP. It was the executive orders that he issued that gave the GOP ammunition to attempt to intimidate and politically bash Obama.

Now that Obama was out of office, Trump and the GOP's frontal attack on his executive orders was much more than an angry and indignant party going after executive orders it didn't like, or to restore what it considered its proper congressional lawmaking authority. It was revenge, pure and simple, against a former president's legacy. Much of that legacy was intertwined with his willingness to use the power of his office whenever and wherever he thought he could to frontally challenge the GOP to cease its relentless, dogged, and destructive campaign of dither, delay, denial, and obstructionism to anything that had the White House stamp on it.

The executive orders on gun control were a textbook example

of that. Another was the executive order that required prospective federal contractors to disclose labor law violations and give federal agencies more guidance on how to consider labor violations when awarding federal contracts. This was a measure that was long past due given both the rampant nepotism, cronyism, game-playing, and outright racial and gender discrimination by an untold number of businesses that grab federal contracts.

These two orders drove home that Obama was determined to make a lasting mark by using federal power in the fight against the gun-related carnage that wracked the nation as well as the blatant racial and gender bias in the workplace. The executive orders on environmental, immigration, and LGBT issues were also landmark measures that would have lasting imprint for his administration. This was anathema to Trump and the GOP. It was why Trump deemed that he'd have to wipe the slate completely clean of the acts of a former president who, in part was popular, and who was widely regarded as a president who cared about the poor and minorities. However, in greater part it was because Obama was seen by many blacks as the fulfillment of their dream of political empowerment and as an historic advance in the battle for civil rights and equality in America. He was not just a president. He was their president. This was what a Trump could not abide. The destruction of Obama's programs, legacy, and ultimately place in history was Trump's obsession for which there was no cure.

CHAPTER 8

The Message to Trump: No Photo-Ops

It was a moment that was tailor made for high TV news drama and continuous looping on that night's news. A black reporter at Trump's White House news conference in February 2017, furiously waves her hand at Trump during the press conference to ask a question. A moment before Trump had brashly said that he had a plan to fix the ills of the inner cities. Trump then recognized her, and without missing a beat, she fires this question at Trump: "When you say the inner cities, are you going to include the CBC (Congressional Black Caucus), Mr. President, in your conversations with your urban agenda, inner city agenda?"

An incredulous Trump fires back "Well I would, tell you what, do you want to set up the meeting?" It was a silly and presumptuous Trump retort. The notion that a reporter had the clout and the *entre* to set up a meeting with an organization of top ranking black congressional representatives was highly problematic. And, not surprisingly, the chair of the CBC, was enraged at the suggestion that a reporter could be a go-between between Trump and the black elected officials.

That wouldn't and couldn't happen. However, Trump had planted the seed with his ludicrous proposal that indeed he was willing to meet with black elected officials, almost all of whom were Democrats, and implacably hostile to any and everything that Trump stood for.

The remarkable exchange between Trump and the black reporter was even more stunning given the checklist of black organizations, groups, and individuals Trump had flatly refused to speak to, reach out to or even acknowledge existed. They included: The NAACP, the National Urban League, The National Association of Black Journalists, black Pastoral groups, and a host of black business groups and entrepreneurs in Detroit. His cold-shoulder of blacks during the campaign even puzzled Gregory Cheadle. He was the man who Trump had famously called "my African-American" at a campaign rally in Redding, California in June 2016. Cheadle, like blacks within and without Trump's campaign, had begged him to at least make some nod toward black voters.

He gave not the slightest hint that he'd meet with them in the year he was running for president. There were good reasons why. He had worked too hard to get his consistent poll readings of a meagre 1 percent of black voter support. This was the percent of black voters polls showed he'd garner in the election. He could not risk his standing with conservative white voters to risk that by giving some face time to a few black groups. He worked harder than any GOP presidential candidate since maybe Reagan in 1980 to ensure that black voters roundly rejected his candidacy.

His 1 percent black support reinforced his standing as the presidential candidate who would not kowtow to blacks to his most rabid backers. They were fearful, conservative white blue-collar workers, and a solid slice of equally frustrated white middle-class suburban voters. They were the ones who packed his mass rallies, and screamed at, and about, liberals, belt way politicians, and President Obama, tanking the economy, cutting unfair trade deals with China, eviscerating their working and middle class living standards, giving away the company store in entitlements to minorities, and turning America's borders into sieves for any and every immigrant type to illegally sneak in. The few blacks who turned up at his rallies seemed to be either bought and paid for acolytes or were there to disrupt them.

Then there was Trump's history. He didn't burst onto the nation's and the media's political radar scope and then claw his way to the top of the GOP presidential heap by making nice with blacks. He did it by baiting, hectoring, and name calling blacks. His victims and targets were prospective black renters who he refused to rent too at his apartment complexes in the 1970s, the one-man crusade he waged to plop the Central Park Five in the gas chamber, the relentless birther smearing of Obama, and his gleeful name calling and insulting of him.

*　*　*　*　*

There was always a crude, cynical and calculating but simple method to Trump's racial nose thumbing. He reasoned that this would be the big motivator to get the estimated 60 plus percent of the white vote that he'd need to negate the overwhelming majority support that Clinton would get from black and Hispanic voters in the 2016 presidential contest. He also needed to pad that by getting disaffected ultra-conservatives, right wing evangelicals, and unreconstructed bigots back to the polls. Many of whom sat out the last two presidential elections because they just couldn't stomach what they considered the "moderate" pabulum that 2008 GOP presidential candidate John McCain and 2012 GOP presidential candidate Mitt Romney dished out.

Trump defiantly broke with the established tradition of other conservative GOP presidents by deliberately refusing to meet with black leaders and at least make a token appearance at a black confab. GOP presidents and presidential contenders Nixon, even Reagan, and Bush Sr. and especially George W. Bush took great pains to give the appearance that they were not overt racists, and that naked racism was not part of their appeal. This included highly orchestrated, stage managed, photo-ops with black celebrities and sports figures, a handful of key black pitch men and women on the campaign trail with them, and having a pack of show piece, African-Americans to provide entertainment and perfunctory speeches at Republican conventions.

Trump didn't want or need that because it would fly in the face of the narrative and the image that he crafted for his campaign that was stuffed with the GOP's standard use of racially loaded code words and attack points.

* * * * *

Trump's ignoring of blacks on the campaign trail was frustrating and puzzling for his small and long-suffering African-American outreach contingent. They implored him to take a few moments and show up at and say something nice to a black gathering now and then. They got the same brush off. So, it was a relief to them when Trump finally did make his pilgrimage to two black churches in Detroit and Cleveland during the latter stage of the campaign.

It gave hope that Trump would eventually have more highly publicized smiling and back slapping photo-ops at his Trump Tower suites with a few hand-picked black ministers and personalities. This would be his way of saying that "though I won't do anything to get another digit of black support, I'm not really a racist." He'd shrug off the predictable and expected savaging he'd get for it from civil rights groups and Democrats, since the photo-ops weren't intended to make nice with blacks anyway.

Despite Trump's countless signals that black voters weren't and must not be in his campaign equation, he still got calls and requests to show up at black gatherings. It was because many just couldn't believe that in 2016 a major party presidential candidate could not only not make even a feeble attempt to get a few black votes, but that he'd run from those votes like the plague. Trump was that candidate.

However, it was a different ball game once he was elected. There was absolutely no way that he could continue to duck meeting with a group such as the Congressional Black Caucus for two reasons. The black reporter that challenged him to meet with them pointed to one when she reminded him that the CBC members as elected officials were the duly constituted official political voice of African-Americans voters. The other reason was that Trump had to at least make a nod to getting bi-partisan support for his so-called urban agenda. That is, if he was serious about putting proposals on the legislative table to further that agenda that would have any chance of passing. The CBC would have to figure in that White House political strategy.

Trump for once was as good as his word after the exchange with the black reporter at the White House press conference. Within days a March 2017 meeting with the CBC was scheduled. The question then became: What would and should the CBC say to Trump at that meeting?

* * * * *

There was much debate within and without CBC circles about that question. The question struck to the heart of the history and function of the CBC in serving as the political voice of blacks. The black congressional elected officeholders were not the carefully vetted, hand-picked array of former black athletes, rappers, preachers, and conservative black Republicans that Trump paraded up to Trump Tower and then paraded to the front of the building for the mandatory photo-op shoot. The CBC was not the throng of Black College Presidents and administrators who Trump met with at the White House in February 2016 and then posed again for the mandatory photo-op.

The message from the CBC to Trump was that there should be no more empty, cheap photo-ops that did nothing but burnish his dubious image as a man who was ready, willing, and anxious to be the president of all the people. This entailed meeting with black interest groups. There was good reason the CBC wanted to shelve the cameras for its Trump meeting and any other future meetings.

The CBC is a fully engaged political group. They are staunch Democrats. Black congressional representatives marched in near total lockstep with the party, and Democratic presidents, Obama and Clinton, on health care reform; affirmative action; increased government spending on education, jobs, and social programs; tight reins on Wall Street and the banking industry; opposition to endless proposed GOP tax cuts for the rich; and a massive urban reconstruction program. True, many African-Americans carp and take pot shots at the CBC for being too cozy, or handmaidens to the Democrats.

The bitter reality, though, was that despite their frequent complaints about the Democratic Party taking their vote for granted, black voters have been the bedrock of the Democratic Party since the 1960s. They couldn't break ranks with the party even if they wanted too. The Trump win made it even clearer that the Democrats were still the only political game in town when it came to giving political voice to their needs and waging any kind of fight-back against Trump.

The CBC faced the challenge of its political lifetime in confronting Trump's rein in the Oval Office. It would be required to toss its weight around at every turn to try and blunt or beat back some of the worst initiatives that Trump was likely to put on the table from his draconian budget cuts, the hack away at voting rights, the wild expansion of police power, gutting public education for school choice, and a benign neglect of civil rights protections.

Even before his meeting with the CBC, Trump had already indicated that one of his priorities would be to loosen civil rights enforcement in some federal agencies, if not outright disband their enforcement and compliance units. He'd do it by whittling down their funding in the budget he would propose for 2018. A prime example was the Labor Department. He would totally eliminate funding for the unit in the department responsible for policing federal contractors too insure that minorities receive their fair share of contracts and prevent discrimination in hiring. Every department's civil rights enforcement unit would suffer the fate of cutbacks under Trump. The Environmental Protection Agency's Environmental Justice program would go. The Education Department's Office of Civil Rights would be drastically scaled back. The Department of Housing and Urban Development, and the Department of Health and Human Services would also have their units that monitor and investigate civil rights violation complaints cut back or eliminated.

Blacks expected the CBC to tell Trump that they were going to fight him on every turn on these issues. They're also politicians and as politicians if they could find any common ground for negotiation on any of his proposals then so be it. However, Trump was not a Bush or Reagan. They were traditional GOP presidents who played within the rules of the negotiating game with Democrats. Trump was anything but. His budget sent the strong message that he was willing to rip apart the rules of the game to get his way.

Still, Trump quickly found out that all his bluster and executive orders meant little if he couldn't get at least some Democrats to go along with him on some issues. This meant trying to make at least some of its members less combative in opposing him. The two points that even remotely offered any semblance of a negotiating chip between him and the Congressional Black Caucus and other civil rights organizations that would press Trump would be on jobs and how to create more of them in inner-city neighborhoods. He also declared that he believed in and wanted to promote equal justice under the law. This was a crucial area for black leaders to press him on.

The Caucus would have to revamp an argument that it repeatedly used with former President Obama and that's that the administration had to do more, spend more, and create more job and skills training programs that targeted young African-American males. They have the chronically suffered more than any other group from poverty and unemployment.

The Caucus could make this issue along with the devastating impact that scrapping much of Obamacare would have on the black poor priority issues in meetings and dealings they had with Trump. Just how many of those there would be in the future was anybody's guess? The CBC was certainly as far removed from Trump's support base as the sun and the moon. That separation was not likely to be closed by one meeting. It certainly wouldn't be closed by turning any meetings it had with him into a Trump photo-op.

* * * * *

So, then what exactly could the CBC's executive board members get out of Trump and what did Trump get out of the CBC in their March 2017 meeting? The answer to that would tell much about how and what relationship blacks would have with Trump during his tenure in the White House. The first discordant note was struck not by those who showed up for the meeting. But by those who didn't.

Many of the CBC members openly said they would not attend. The second bad note was struck in the seating arrangement in the meeting room for the executive board members who did attend. They deliberately sat out of camera view with him. As CBC member, Rep. Donald A. McEachin (D-Va.), who did not attend the meeting pointedly noted, "The Congressional Black Caucus is not going to be a potted plant or a photo opportunity. He did a photo op with the presidents of historically black colleges, and they got nothing."

Trump for his part gushed for the reporters and cameras over his supposed profound respect for the work of the CBC, "They've lifted up the conscience of our nation in the march toward civil rights, enriched the soul of America in their faith and courage, and they've advanced our country in the fields of science, arts and medicine."

Despite the platitude, the CBC had no illusions that Trump would offer anything tangible in the way of a commitment toward strengthening civil rights enforcement, or more funding and support for jobs and health care programs. The policy memo the black legislators brought with them, "A Lot to Lose," was a deliberate play on his shout at a campaign rally during the campaign that blacks had nothing to lose by bolting from the Democrats. Their memo was mostly ignored by him. The best that could be hoped for as one CBC member at the meeting said was that they would have a "candid" talk. It wasn't clear whether that happened. However, in the end, Trump did get the photo-op the CBC dreaded. The White House tweeted a photo of them together.

Trump at least for the moment wouldn't get a second chance to tweet out another photo of he and CBC members sitting around the table at the White House in a meeting. In June 2017, three months after the March meeting, the CBC publicly declined a second meeting with Trump. In a public letter responding to the invitation to meet, the CBC minced no words, "We have seen no evidence that your administration acted on our calls for action, and we have in fact witnessed steps that will affirmatively hurt black communities." The black legislators ticked off the hideous list of Trump actions that "hurt" blacks. They included his proposed massive budget cuts to job and education programs, the ramp up on the war on drugs, and the slash and burn of health care. The CBC did leave the door for future engagement with Trump slightly ajar by indicating that he could meet with individual members when the need arose.

The best then that could be said about the March meeting then was that an embarrassed Trump finally met with black leaders. And a few black leaders swallowed their distaste for him, and met with him. That didn't say much about how blacks would navigate the dangerous Trump waters during his White House years.

However, the CBC and seven other major civil rights organizations did give a tangible sign how they'd combat those waters when it announced it would battle hard in Congress and the courts to block Trump's draconian 2018 health, education, social services and job funding cuts. This would almost certainly be the pattern during Trump's White House stay. He would propose legislation or an initiative that would eviscerate or defund a civil rights, labor, or criminal justice reform program or initiative and the CBC and civil rights groups would quickly respond. Their response would be angry press conferences denouncing the action, an occasional march, and where feasible taking the matter to the courts. In essence, it marked a return to the kind of civil rights activism that was the trademark of the 1960s. To do less would sink blacks even deeper in the dangerous Trump waters. It would take more than photo-ops to prevent that.

CHAPTER 9

The Trump Challenge

At campaign rallies in August and September 2016, in two different states, Michigan and Virginia, Trump blasted the Democratic Party and blacks for their rock-solid loyalty to the party. At the Virginia rally, he put it bluntly, "What do you have to lose by trying something new, like Trump? You're living in your poverty, your schools are no good, you have no jobs, 58 percent of your youth is unemployed—what the hell do you have to lose?" The audiences at both rallies were almost all white. So, he may have been talking about blacks. But he was talking to whites since blacks weren't there to hear him.

Nonetheless, no matter who the audience was and what his message to them was, the hottest conversation during, and after his campaign, and White House win, was how a President Trump would govern. There was much speculation, many hints, lots of innuendos, and even great terror about that. Blacks were among those at the top of the public interest group pyramid who worried the most about a Trump White House. The prime cause of their deep fear was that they would have the most to lose with Trump in the Oval Office.

There was consensus, though, that a Trump White House would

be radically different then just about any other White House in de-cades. There was also consensus about Trump's style. That he would translate his make America great campaign slogan into a slash and burn policy aimed at an array of Obama era education, civil rights, job, and criminal justice reform programs. There was much agree-ment among Trump's opponents that he was ill-suited to patient, give-and-take negotiation and compromise to get his initiatives through Congress. His style would be to bellow, bully, and harangue to get his way.

Before the election, Trump had been on the political scene long enough to leave enough of a paper trail to piece together from his statements in debates, interviews, and speeches, a fairly accurate pic-ture of what he would say and do on the big-ticket issues all of which impacted blacks once in the White House. Those issues were the budget, government spending, civil rights enforcement, the environ-ment, crime control, the military, and foreign policy.

*   *   *   *   *

He'd be totally hands-off Wall Street and the banks on regu-latory matters, slash corporate taxes to "0" percent, impose no cap and tax on big oil, and radically slash funding for the EPA and the Department of Education. The one department that would not be put on a starvation funding diet would be the Pentagon. The Defense De-partment would get a massive boost in funding and a virtual green light on any military action it deemed necessary to protect America's security. This could mean putting boots on the ground against ISIS, taking a hardline confrontational stance in confronting North Korea and Iran on their nuclear capacity.

On the surface, these seemed race neutral issues. However, they were anything but. Billions of dollars more for defense, cuts in fund-

ing for education and environmental protection would inevitably
translate into cuts for civil rights enforcement and compliance programs and the loosening of regulations on toxic wastes and pollution
controls in those departments in order to pay for a further bloated
military. The gut of regulations reining in Wall Street and banking
industry abuses would invariably mean few checks on corporate
abuses against consumers. They could include everything from business and housing lending to investments. Those suffering the most
from those abuses and the cutbacks in domestic agency departments
would be blacks, Hispanics, and the poor.

Trump's avowed aim to appoint more strict constructionist
judges to the Supreme Court and the federal judiciary in the mode of
Scalia could mean a rollback of the major gains in labor, civil rights,
voting rights, and civil liberties protections. It would also give free
rein to corporations to roll back labor and employee rights. The appointment of a conservative to run the Justice Department would ef-
fectively mean minorities and the poor could no longer look to that
department as its dependable line of defense to protect against rights
abuses and police violence. The short and long-term effect of this
would be to further speed up the school to prison pipeline for many
young blacks.

The two policy areas that Trump left no doubt during the campaign that he would make priority items were the elimination of
Obamacare which would drive tens of millions back into the ranks
of the uninsured with all its disastrous health and cost consequences.
This would ignite yet another profound health crisis in providing access to affordable health care and treatment for millions of blacks.

The other policy area that Trump would move quickly to take
action on was Obama's executive orders. He would try to wipe out
any of his orders that had anything remotely to do with health, edu-

cation, criminal justice, tougher corporate regulations, and environmental protections. On the signature issues that got him raves from millions during the campaign, he'd do everything to further erode labor unions, flatly oppose any minimum wage increase, try to wall off the borders, and crack down on Muslims coming and going in the country. He was as good as his words on the Muslim ban. Despite several court rebukes striking down his Muslim ban, he blustered ahead with it and almost certainly would spend even more time, administration resources, and sow more public rancor over it by trying to push it all the way to the Supreme Court.

During the campaign, Trump didn't lay down a specific blueprint for how he'd work with Congressional Democrats or even Congressional Republicans, let alone foreign leaders, if elected. There was really no need to do that at that point. It would have ham strung his free-wheeling, shoot from the lip approach to campaigning. If anything, the absence of such a blueprint added to his take-no-prisoners, tough talk, rip the establishment, allure among conservative voters.

* * * * *

Trump's hyped up, disgruntled, vengeful backers, all saw this as the prescription for a new type of White House—and better still, a change in the substance and style of governance. However, for blacks it was the diametric opposite. It was a deeply perilous challenge that would require new tactics, strategies, and activism that characterized the civil rights movement of the 1960s. The task of such a new civil rights movement's would be to fight back against the danger that Trump posed to all the hard-fought gains blacks made during the latter part of the 20th Century and into the 21st Century.

The terrifying reality was that barring a political miracle, a Trump impeachment and resignation was little more than wishful thinking and a fond hope. In any case, it was no substitute for hard work, persistent activist organizing, and holding black and Democratic elected officials accountable in opposing Trump and the GOP's attempt to gut everything from education to health care to civil rights. The new movement would have to place major emphasis on getting out the vote in as great, if not greater numbers, in the mid-term election in 2018 and the presidential election in 2020 as turned out in 2008 and 2012 to put and keep Obama in the White House with all the energy, resources, and political tools that could be mustered. This time the goal would be to elect Democrats at the state and congressional level committed to doing fierce legislative battle against Trump's wrecking ball policies.

The Trump challenge was real and more serious than many blacks could ever imagine in their worst nightmare. Nonetheless, it was a challenge that had to be faced, confronted, and overcome.

CHAPTER 10

Democrats to the Rescue?

The mood was raucous and joyous when a beaming newly elected President Trump stepped to the stage in Grand Rapids, Michigan on December 9, 2016. This was Trump country, and a Trump crowd like nearly all others before, during, and after the presidential campaign. It was white, suburban, and more male than female. This was the first leg of what Trump billed as his "thank you" victory tour across the country. He dutifully thanked the crowd there for their backing. However, he also had thanks for another group, black voters.

"The African American community was great to us," gushed Trump, "They came through big league. And frankly, if they had any doubt, they didn't vote. And that was almost as good. Because a bunch of people didn't show up, because they felt good about me." There it was. Trump thanking blacks not for voting against him, but for not voting at all. It was, rude, insulting and hyperbole of the highest order. However, there was a hard, bitter element of perverse truth in his gloating dig at black voters and, by implication, the Democratic Party.

As they had for every election since 1964, black voters gave their majority vote to the Democratic presidential candidate in 2016. Clinton got nearly 90 percent of the black vote. However, the real story as Trump perversely noted were the voters who didn't show up. The final vote tabulation showed a drop-off in the black vote in major urban areas from the 2008 and 2016 presidential elections. Michigan was a sad example of that. Obama easily won the state twice. Clinton barely lost it. Clearly, a lot of blacks who packed the polls twice with passion and exuberance for Obama, stayed home on election day in 2016. The story was the same across the country.

The black vote dropped 7 percent in 2016 from what it was in 2008 and 2012. That nudged the overall black voter percentage of the overall American electorate down 1 percent. Trump's margin of victory was less than 100,000 in the three states that tipped it to him, Pennsylvania, Wisconsin, and Michigan. Obama won all three in 2008 and 2012. That 1 percent drop, and the 7 percent drop in the black vote total in 2016, helped seal Clinton's election doom. Why and How did that happen given the monumental stakes in the election, the dire peril that Trump posed to civil rights, health care, and criminal justice reform, jobs, and education, the issues that blacks most cared about and affected them more than any other group?

* * * * *

In fairness, there was never much chance that Clinton could match the euphoria and history making candidacy and presidency of Obama. He was seen not as a distant, remote, traditional presidential candidate, but almost as a family member—someone to embrace and take personal pride in their accomplishments. Many blacks in the past were apathetic, lethargic and indifferent to the political process because they thought their vote made no difference, or because of their antipathy to the Democrats, whom they accused of plantationism. That is the notion that Democrats hold blacks in a kind of political captivity by taking their vote for granted while supposedly giving little in return.

Clinton's apparent big advantage to attain close to the same overall percentage of the black vote as Obama got in 2012 was Trump. His naked race baiting, polarizing digs, insults, cracks and history of bigotry against blacks quickly materialized in some polls showing him getting zero percent of the black vote. His few showy, media photo-op spectacles at a few handpicked black churches with a thoroughly sanitized audience, fooled no one, and simply added more insult to injury with blacks.

The story wouldn't have been much different for any other GOP presidential candidate. In fact, the GOP's bigotry would always have been one of her greatest strengths and selling points with black voters, as it has been for Democrats the past half century. During this time, every GOP presidential candidate has gotten no more than a marginal percentage of the overall black vote. Its half century of race baiting, racial exclusion and relentless and brutal assaults on affirmative action, voting rights, civil rights protections—along with a near eight-year, unbroken record of hectoring, harassing and obstructing every program under Obama—has earned it the undying enmity of black voters.

The lip service by the Republican National Committee in 2012 about making the GOP a more diverse and inclusive party bumped hard against the brutal political reality that the GOP was rightly regarded as a nesting ground for bigots, extremists and assorted racial haters. It has relied on them to be its back-door shock troops to rally millions of backers in the South and the Heartland in elections.

The prevailing thinking then was that it wouldn't take Obama, not being the White House candidate, though, for blacks to turn out on Election Day 2016 in sufficient numbers to give Clinton the edge in the key swing states. Lawsuits were filed in North Carolina, Ohio and Pennsylvania alleging that the GOP was up to its usual vote suppression tricks. One of the lawsuits in North Carolina was successful. This would help clear some of the barriers to black voting in these states. The ease of early voting in other states would also insure that adequate numbers of black voters cast a ballot.

All then Clinton had to do is what Democrats have done in presidential elections for the last half century, and that was to be regarded as a good Democrat. It seemed this would be more than enough to ensure that the black vote would still be Clinton's key to the Oval Office.

That assumption fell flat on its face. The starting, and sadly, ending point for that to the party's embarrassment was the Democratic Party. The seeds of the Party's collapse in 2016 were planted ironically during the Bill Clinton White House years in the 1990s.

Clinton radically downsized welfare, toughened federal anti-crime and drug laws, and pared away affirmative action programs. These were all Reagan, Bush Sr. and Nixon proposals that the Congressional Black Caucus and liberal Democrats vehemently opposed, and had languished in Congress. The ranks of the black poor quickly soared, the numbers jailed for mostly non-violent, non-serious crimes jumped, and funds for skill and education programs to permanently break the welfare cycle for the poor evaporated.

Clinton did appoint a handful of blacks to administration positions and increased funding for AIDS prevention, minority business, education, and African relief. But Bush did pretty much the same thing.

Democratic presidential candidates Al Gore in 2004, and John Kerry in 2004, spent most of their losing presidential campaigns avoiding appearances in black communities. They were silent on issues such as racial profiling, affirmative action, housing and job discrimination, the racial disparities in prison sentencing, the HIV/AIDS epidemic, health care for the poor, failing inner city schools, and ending the racially-marred drug sentencing policy.

They got away with this by playing hard on the terror and panic that a Bush White House win in 2000 and his reelection in 2004 stirred in many blacks. But when blacks scurried to vote for Gore and Kerry out of fear of a Bush win they gave the Democrats another free ride.

Despite the major policy initiatives of the Obama administration, health care, criminal justice reforms, and boosts in education and job spending that paid dividends for blacks, Obama at times followed the cautious, moderate Democratic script. He talked tough talk about ramping up military and intelligence spending, making hard target preemptive strikes, and a massive troop build-up in Afghanistan. This was a transparent effort to out war hawk the GOP on their pet national security issue. It was also a big tip off that military preparedness and national security, not civil rights or social issues would remain the Democrat's prime campaign focus.

The wrinkle that Obama added to the campaign which ultimately tipped the scales to him was the economy. He ripped a page straight out of the Clinton playbook and pledged big tax breaks for the middle-class. That did two things. It sent a strong signal that the Democrats could also pitch the virtues of the middle-class. It sent the more subtle signal that Democrats would continue to place priority on middle-class needs and concerns, and not those of the black poor. This caused unease and even conflict at times between Obama and the Congressional Black Caucus. The specific issue was the chronic, and astronomical unemployment rate among young black males.

* * * * *

In a press interview in March 2010, Obama bluntly said that he would not propose any special initiatives for blacks. His sharp retort was in direct response to questions about whether he'd propose any special initiatives to deal with their stubbornly high joblessness. By then the figures on black male unemployment matched and, in some parts of the country, topped the unemployment rate at the height of the 1930s Great Depression.

The Congressional Black Caucus demanded that Obama specifically shell out more money and formulate more programs to help the black jobless and to aid cash strapped minority broadcasters and minority businesses. The Caucus lightly saber rattled Obama with the threat of delaying or even opposing his financial regulation plan if he didn't play ball. The Caucus was not going to oppose Obama on his proposed bill. But it made its point. And so did Obama when he reiterated that he wouldn't propose any new programs for blacks.

The dilemma that black Democrats faced was that they had to wage a dual fight. The first was for their black constituents. The other was to get anything meaningful through Congress and state legislatures that protected those interests in the vital areas of jobs, education, housing, and civil rights protections. Their heavy reliance on the muscle and structure of the Democratic Party required that they be party team players, first and foremost. Obama's refusal to propose any special initiatives to combat black joblessness had everything to do with the price of White House governance, and party allegiance. Obama as the party's titular head and top Democrat, as

Bill Clinton successfully, and Gore and Kerry unsuccessfully, did made a deliberate and politically calculated decision that strong security and middle-class tax and economic relief was the only way to beat the GOP for the White House. Any hint of a tilt toward minorities by Democrats would be political suicide. Unfortunately, this didn't do much for the black poor and working class. Without Obama on the presidential ticket, that political vulnerability could pose peril to the Democrats. Much would depend on just how effective the party was in getting the message out that it wanted and needed black votes to win, and to craft a boots on the ground outreach plan to sell black voters on that. It would take hard work. The big part of that work fell on the shoulders of the Democratic National Committee. It fumbled the ball badly.

*　*　*　*　*

The Democratic National Committee was by any standard a wreck and a ruin during the 2016 presidential campaign. It got pounded for misstep after misstep that included: poor, and disconnected leadership, leaked emails, gross favoritism, petty infighting, blatant manipulation of the primaries, and gross cluelessness about the Trump threat.

The Democratic National Committee is tasked with the chore of spotting and recruiting able talent to run as Democrats for office, then helping to raise money for the Democratic candidates and incumbents, putting volunteer and paid professional organizers on the ground for their campaigns, and mounting an all-out get out the vote blitz in the weeks leading up to the election to put Democrats locally and nationally over the top.

This takes a well-oiled, well-coordinated ground game to put as many Democrats as possible in Congress and to keep the ones who are there in Congress. The even bigger challenge is to hold its base in line; a key part of that vase is black voters.

Many of them were missing from the polls in 2016. An even greater number of them were no-shows in the 2010 and 2014 midterm elections.

The other bitter truth is that Trump won many disconnected and frustrated white voters by welding their latent racist, anti-immigrant, anti-woman, pseudo patriotic sentiment to their loathing of, and alienation from, the GOP and the Democrat's, disconnect with America's Main Street. That's a tough hurdle for a progressive or a centrist Democrat to overcome. The better option for the DNC and the Democratic Party remained to pad the number of Hispanics, blacks, women, and youth in the five or six states that elect presidents.

The gaping disparity between the GOP and Democrats in voter turnout in the primaries was not in the tens of thousands, but millions. The GOP energized its base like it hadn't been in years, as well as firing up lots of young persons who in years' past would likely not have been caught dead voting for a GOP presidential candidate. At the same time, the Democratic turnout was to be charitable, tepid.

This again speaks to the Democrats having an effective political ground game that targets blacks. The bitter pill to swallow is that the GOP learned from its defeat in 2008 and went to the basics of how to energize and mobilize its supporters. It was political organizing 101. In a special district race in Georgia in June 2017, the GOP put legions of organizers in the field did lots of canvassing and phoning, paid for digital ads that targeted GOP voters with special emphasis on those who hadn't voted in a prior election. It paid off. The GOP candidate won the seat. The entire focus on the effort was to target traditional GOP voters. They are white, male, suburban, and rural, blue collar, and lower middle-class voters. The party tailored its appeals to their interests. The same playbook must be employed with blacks. If not, black voters will not respond in large enough numbers to offset the GOP vote base in the key swing states.

The universal consensus is that future elections will come down to which party can get the greatest number of voters to the polls to vote for their candidate in every race from the White House to congressional and statewide offices. It's a numbers game pure and simple. In the 2014 midterms, and in the states Trump needed to win in 2016, the GOP showed that it could get those numbers out. The Democrats task is to do the same. However, if significant numbers of black voters in urban areas in perennial swing states such as Ohio, Pennsylvania, Michigan and Florida, North Carolina feel that the party does not give paramount importance to their interests, actively court their vote, and craft programs and initiatives on everything from joblessness to civil rights, waving the Trump and the GOP threat in front of their collective faces won't be enough to get them to the polls and pull the Democratic candidate lever.

The question is can and will the Democrats be able to make their numbers bulge over the GOP and the rage at Trump mean something? This is the big question and challenge for the Democratic Party.

Be the Judge: Trump's 10-Point Plan for Black America

At a campaign rally in Akron, Ohio in November 2016, Trump did what many blacks thought was unthinkable for him. He unveiled a plan that he claimed would remake black America. It covered many of the compelling public policy concerns that directly impacted on blacks. But there were two questions dangling about his ten-point plan for blacks. The first was, was he for real in trying to implement all or part of the plan? The other question was would it work if he really was serious about it? In this case, here's the plan, be the judge.

1. Great Education Through School Choice. We will allow every disadvantaged child in America to attend the public, private, charter, magnet, religious or home school of their choice. School choice is the great civil rights issue of our time, and Donald Trump will be the nation's biggest cheerleader for school choice in all 50 states. We will also ensure funding for Historic Black Colleges and

Universities, more affordable 2- and 4-year college, and support for trade and vocational education.

2. Safe Communities. We will make our communities safe again. Every poor African-American child must be able to walk down the street in peace. Safety is a civil right. We will invest in training and funding both local and federal law enforcement operations to remove the gang members, drug dealers, and criminal cartels from our neighborhoods. The reduction of crime is not merely a goal – but a necessity.

3. Equal Justice Under the Law. We will apply the law fairly, equally and without prejudice. There will be only one set of rules – not a two-tiered system of justice. Equal justice also means the same rules for Wall Street.

4. Tax Reforms to Create Jobs and Lift up People and Communities. We will lower the business tax from 35 percent to 15 percent and bring thousands of new companies to our shores. We will also have a massive middle-class tax cut, tax-free childcare savings accounts, and childcare tax deductions and credits.

We will also have tax holidays for inner-city investment, and new tax incentives to get foreign companies to relocate in blighted American neighborhoods. We will empower cities and states to seek a federal disaster designation for blighted communities in order to initiate the rebuilding of vital infrastructure, the demolition of abandoned properties, and the increased presence of law enforcement.

5. Financial Reforms to Expand Credit to Support New Job Creation. We will have financial reforms to make it easier for young African-Americans to get credit to pursue their dreams in business and create jobs in their communities. Dodd-Frank (note: The toughened consumer protection regulations) has been a disaster, making it harder for small businesses to get the credit they need.

The policies of the Clintons brought us the financial recession – through lifting Glass-Steagall (note: the banking deregulation act passed during the Clinton era), pushing subprime lending, and blocking reforms to Fannie and Freddie. It's time for a 21st century Glass-Steagall and, as part of that, a priority on helping African-American businesses get the credit they need. We will also encourage small-business creation by allowing social welfare workers to convert poverty assistance into repayable but forgiven micro-loans.

6. Trade That Works for American Workers. We will stop the massive, chronic trade deficits that have emptied out our jobs. We won't let our jobs be stolen from us anymore. We will stop the off-shoring of companies to low-wage countries and raise wages at home – meaning rent and bills become instantly more affordable. We will tell executives that if they move their factories to Mexico or other countries, we will put a 35% tax on their product before they ship it back into the United States.

7. Protection from Illegal Immigration. We will restore the civil rights of African-Americans, Hispanic-Americans, and all Americans, by ending illegal immigration. No group has been more economically harmed by decades of illegal immigration than low-income African-American workers.

Hillary's pledge to enact "open borders," – made in secret to a foreign bank – would destroy the African-American middle class. We will reform visa rules to give American workers preference for jobs, and we will suspend reckless refugee admissions from terror-prone regions that cost taxpayers hundreds of billions of dollars. We will use a portion of the money saved by enforcing our laws, and suspending refugees, to re-invested in our inner cities.

8. New Infrastructure Investment. We will leverage public-private partnerships, and private investments through tax incentives, to spur $1 trillion in infrastructure investment over 10 years, of which the inner cities will be a major beneficiary. We will cancel all wasteful climate change spending from Obama-Clinton, including all global warming payments to the United Nations. This will save $100 billion over 8 years. We will use these to help rebuild the vital infrastructure, including water systems, in America's inner cities.

9. Protect the African-American Church. We will protect religious liberty, promote strong families, and support the African-American church.

10. America First Foreign Policy. We will stop trying to build democracies overseas, wasting trillions, but focus on defeating terrorists and putting America First.

Be the judge!

Notes

Introduction

https://www.si.com/nfl/2016/12/13/ray-lewis-jim-brown-donald-trump-meeting-trump-tower

http://www.eurweb.com/2016/12/jim-brown-blames-typo-says-hes-not-love-donald-trump/

https://www.nytimes.com/interactive/2017/01/13/us/politics/trump-cabinet-women-minorities.html?_r=0

http://www.huffingtonpost.com/earl-ofari-hutchinson/i-fell-in-love-with-trump_b_13677550.html

Chapter 1

http://www.cnn.com/2015/11/22/politics/donald-trump-black-lives-matter-protester-confrontation/index.html

http://abcnews.go.com/Politics/donald-trump-announces-2016-presidential-campaign-make-country/story?id=31799741

https://www.theguardian.com/us-news/2016/feb/17/central-park-five-donald-trump-jogger-rape-case-new-york

https://www.washingtonpost.com/politics/inside-the-governments-racial-bias-case-against-donald-trumps-company-and-how-he-fought-it/2016/01/23/fb90163e-bfbe-11e5-bcda-62a36b394160_story.html?utm_term=.d3705e9e9974

http://www.npr.org/2016/09/29/495955920/donald-trump-plagued-by-decades-old-housing-discrimination-case

https://www.nytimes.com/2016/09/17/us/politics/donald-trump-obama-birther.html?_r=0

http://www.cbssports.com/nba/news/donald-trump-donald-sterling-was-set-up-by-girlfriend-from-hell/

https://www.nytimes.com/2016/09/22/us/politics/donald-trump-don-king-black-voters.html?_r=0

http://www.huffingtonpost.com/earl-ofari-hutchinson/trump-steals-nixons-law-a_b_10975322.html

Chapter 2

http://www.pbs.org/wgbh/pages/frontline/shows/jesus/evangelicals/bushand.html

http://www.npr.org/2015/12/01/457930597/black-pastor-calls-trump-meeting-a-get-played-moment

https://www.washingtonpost.com/news/monkey-cage/wp/2016/11/11/trump-got-more-votes-from-people-of-color-than-romney-did-heres-the-data/?utm_term=.45c612bb6789

https://www.nytimes.com/2016/04/18/us/politics/hillary-bill-clinton-crime-bill.html?_r=0

http://www.nytimes.com/2013/05/23/opinion/blow-blacks-conservatives-and-plantations.html

http://www.broadcastingcable.com/news/washington/trump-meets-bet-founder-bob-johnson/161293

Chapter 3

https://www.aclu.org/files/sessions/010417-SessionsFeature.pdf

https://www.prisonlegalnews.org/news/2017/jan/13/analysis-sen-jeff-sessionss-record-criminal-justice/

https://www.justice.gov/jmd/organization-mission-and-func-tions-manual-attorney-general

http://www.cnn.com/2016/12/21/politics/jeff-sessions-prosecu-torial-misconduct/index.html

https://www.thenation.com/article/jeff-sessions-has-spent-his-whole-career-opposing-voting-rights/

http://prospect.org/article/22-states-wave-new-voting-restric-tions-threatens-shift-outcomes-tight-races

https://www.justice.gov/opa/pr/attorney-general-sessions-di-rects-federal-prosecutors-target-most-significant-violent

http://www.nbcnews.com/news/us-news/private-prisons-here-s-why-sessions-memo-matters-n725316

http://www.huffingtonpost.com/tony-newman/obama-holder-criminal-justice-reform_b_4775811.html

http://www.drugpolicy.org/race-and-drug-war

http://www.nbcnews.com/storyline/americas-heroin-epidemic/opioid-epidemic-trump-set-commission-addiction-crisis-sources-say-n739861

http://publiceye.org/defendingjustice/pdfs/chapters/tough-crime.pdf

http://www.foxnews.com/politics/2016/07/12/trump-calls-black-lives-matter-divisive-criticizes-police-shootings.html

http://www.cnn.com/2017/04/03/politics/sessions-police-re-form-review/index.html

http://dailycaller.com/2015/05/28/doj-police-probes-and-con-sent-decrees-spike-under-obama/

Chapter 4

http://www.lifenews.com/2016/08/02/donald-trump-i-will-pick-great-supreme-court-justices-like-antonin-scalia/

https://www.nytimes.com/2016/02/13/opinion/justice-antonin-scalias-supreme-court-legacy.html?_r=0

http://www.cnn.com/2016/02/22/politics/clarence-thomas-antonin-scalia-supreme-court/index.html

http://www.nbcconnecticut.com/news/politics/Mike-Pence-Rallies-Michigan—388613102.html

https://www.usatoday.com/story/news/politics/elections/2015/10/25/supreme-court-president-age-80-election/74003698/

http://abcnews.go.com/Politics/hobby-lobby-wins-contraceptive-ruling-supreme-court/story?id=24364311

http://thefederalist.com/2016/07/06/obama-has-lost-in-the-supreme-court-more-than-any-modern-president/

http://www.huffingtonpost.com/adam-winkler/supreme-court-obama_b_1619369.html

http://www.huffingtonpost.com/2013/06/26/supreme-court-prop-8_n_3434854.html

http://www.cnn.com/2016/05/18/politics/donald-trump-supreme-court-nominees/index.html

http://www.cnn.com/2017/01/31/politics/neil-gorsuch-antonin-scalia/index.html

http://scholarlycommons.law.case.edu/cgi/viewcontent.cgi?article=4658&context=caselrev

http://www.latimes.com/politics/la-na-pol-constitution-originalism-20170317-story.html

http://www.politico.com/story/2017/01/who-is-neil-gorsuch-bio-facts-background-political-views-234437

http://www.huffingtonpost.com/entry/thomas-is-not-scalias-clone-hes-thomass_us_58d52f0ae4b0f633072b36bf

http://www.huffingtonpost.com/earl-ofari-hutchinson/how-about-four-more-scali_b_11285596.html

http://www.huffingtonpost.com/earl-ofari-hutchinson/the-supreme-courts-savage_b_5550089.html

Chapter 5

http://www.thegatewaypundit.com/2017/02/president-trump-meets-black-college-presidents-media-focuses-white-aide-taking-pictures/

https://www.washingtonpost.com/graphics/politics/trump-presidential-budget-2018-proposal/?utm_term=.c3535806d610

https://newsone.com/3710695/donald-trump-hbcu-government-spending-bill/

http://www.newyorker.com/news/daily-comment/betsy-devos-and-the-plan-to-break-public-schools

https://www.washingtonpost.com/news/answer-sheet/wp/2016/07/15/how-charter-schools-in-michigan-have-hurt-traditional-public-schools-new-research-finds/?utm_term=.54923666170b

https://www.washingtonpost.com/blogs/govbeat/wp/2013/10/15/charter-schools-are-hurting-urban-public-schools-moodys-says/?utm_term=.568d0dea57eb

http://www.csmonitor.com/USA/Education/2010/0629/Study-On-average-charter-schools-do-no-better-than-public-schools

https://www.washingtonpost.com/news/answer-sheet/wp/2017/04/13/trumps-budget-boosts-funding-for-school-choice-so-why-are-charter-school-chiefs-unhappy-about-it/?utm_term=.5c10e07356a6

https://www.theatlantic.com/news/archive/2017/05/betsy-de-vos-booed-by-students-at-historically-black-university/526197/

http://www.cnn.com/2016/12/05/politics/ben-carson-hud-sec-retary-nomination/index.html

https://www.theguardian.com/us-news/2017/jun/07/ben-car-son-homelessness-donald-trump-budget-cuts

http://www.cbsnews.com/news/ben-carson-expands-on-com-ment-about-poverty-and-state-of-mind/

Chapter 6

https://www.forbes.com/sites/theapothecary/2015/09/28/donald-trump-on-obamacare-on-60-minutes-everybodys-got-to-be-covered-and-the-governments-gonna-pay-for-it/#141f78a5540e

http://dailysignal.com/2015/10/06/how-three-house-commit-tees-plan-to-repeal-parts-of-obamacare/

https://obamacarefacts.com/benefitsofobamacare/

http://jointcenter.org/all-topics/health

http://www.nationalreview.com/article/443604/obamacare-re-peal-fight-how-republicans-can-win

http://www.politico.com/story/2017/01/obamacare-repeal-trump-rand-paul-233351

http://dailysignal.com/2017/02/16/gop-leaders-release-details-of-plan-to-replace-obamacare/

http://www.cnn.com/2017/05/04/politics/health-care-vote/index.html

http://www.cnn.com/2017/06/12/politics/hfr-dennis-rodman-north-korea/index.html?adkey=bn

http://money.cnn.com/2017/05/04/news/economy/republicans-obamacare-repeal-hurt-helped/index.html

Chapter 7

http://www.cnn.com/2015/09/18/politics/trump-obama-muslim-birther/index.html

http://www.cnn.com/2017/03/04/politics/trump-obama-wiretap-tweet/index.html

http://www.huffingtonpost.com/earl-ofari-hutchinson/method-to-racist-madness-_b_3749451.html

http://www.cnn.com/2016/09/15/politics/donald-trump-obama-birther-united-states/

http://www.publicpolicypolling.com/main/2015/08/trump-supporters-think-obama-is-a-muslim-born-in-another-country.html

http://www.huffingtonpost.com/earl-ofari-hutchinson/nail-obamas-executive-ord_b_14304820.html

Chapter 8

http://www.politico.com/story/2017/02/trump-congressional-black-caucus-april-ryan-235102

https://www.washingtonpost.com/politics/trump-administration-plans-to-minimize-civil-rights-efforts-in-agencies/2017/05/29/922fc1b2-39a7-11e7-a058-ddbb23c75d82_story.html?utm_term=.5512b2925a37

http://www.npr.org/2017/03/22/521056894/trump-meets-with-congressional-black-caucus-members

https://www.washingtonpost.com/politics/congressional-black-caucus-leaders-meet-with-trump-push-for-policy-proposals-not-photo-ops/2017/03/22/6cb0e6e6-0f40-11e7-9d5a-a83e627dc120_story.html?utm_term=.d303f1f3cd9b

https://www.blackaids.org/news-2017/3030-cbc-civil-rights-groups-fight-trumps-budget-blueprint

https://www.blackaids.org/news-2017/3030-cbc-civil-rights-groups-fight-trumps-budget-blueprint

https://www.theguardian.com/us-news/2017/jun/21/donald-trump-congressional-black-caucus-no-meeting

Chapter 9

https://www.nytimes.com/2016/08/25/us/politics/donald-trump-black-voters.html?_r=0

http://www.huffingtonpost.com/earl-ofari-hutchinson/heres-how-president-trump_b_8875776.html

http://abcnews.go.com/Politics/trump-white-house/story?id=43215371

Chapter 10

https://thinkprogress.org/trump-black-voters-didnt-vote-92316ddd0400

http://www.politico.com/story/2017/05/10/black-election-turn-out-down-2016-census-survey-238226

http://www.huffingtonpost.com/earl-ofari-hutchinson/hillary-isnt-obama-but-sh_b_12759254.html

http://www.huffingtonpost.com/earl-ofari-hutchinson/obama-again-reminds-hes-n_b_385678.html

Postscript

https://blackamericaweb.com/2016/11/13/donald-trumps-10-point-plan-for-black-america-will-it-work/

http://www.standard.net/National/2017/01/20/Trump-s-10-point-plan-to-help-black-America-doesn-t-look-like-much-of-a-deal

Index

L
Lewis, Ray, 1-3

M
Medicaid under fire from GOP, 66-67
McCain, John, 15, 16, 31, 78
McConnell, Mitch, 14-15, 42

N
Nixon, Richard, 9, 12, 16
    1968 presidential campaign and law and order, 13
    Southern Strategy, 12-13

O
Obama, Barack, 8, 33, 36, 41, 89, 93, 94, 96, 98
    Baited as a Muslim, anti-American, 70-71
    Birtherism attacks, 68-69
    GOP and Trump aim to roll-back Obama programs and legacy, 72
    Receives a minority of white votes in 2008, 2012, 15
    Supreme Court blocks Obama initiatives, 42-43

P
Pence, Mike, 39
Police shootings of African-Americans, 10, 35, 36

R
Reagan, Ronald, 3, 23-24, 29, 31, 74
Republican National Committee, 94
Romney, Mitt, 31, 78

S
Scalia, Antonin, 38
    Trump calls him model judge, 38-39, 40, 42-43
    Scalia and conservative judge's strict constructionism, 40

About the Author

Earl Ofari Hutchinson is an author and political analyst. He is an associate editor of New America Media. He is a long-time blogger for the Huff Post. He is an occasional commentator on race and politics on CNN. He is the author of numerous books on race and politics in America. His most recent books include the trilogy on the Obama Years: *The Obama Legacy, How Obama Governed; The Year of Crisis and Challenge*, and *How Obama Won*.

He is a weekly co-host of the Al Sharpton Show on Radio One. He is the host of the weekly *Hutchinson Report* on KPFK 90.7 FM Los Angeles and the Pacifica Network.

www.ingramcontent.com/pod-product-compliance
Lightning Source LLC
Chambersburg PA
CBHW061148040426
42445CB00013B/1606